NEWS STORIES

October 2023

For Ward Wilson,

a fellow writer,

Peter Uhn

NEWS STORIES

A Memoir

PETER NOLAN

Columbus, Ohio

NEWS STORIES

Published by Gatekeeper Press
2167 Stringtown Rd, Suite 109
Columbus, OH 43123
www.GatekeeperPress.com

ISBN: 9781642370034
eISBN: 9781642370041

Printed in the United States of America

For my Parents,
Ralph and Geraldine Nolan

In memory of
Dan Houlihan, Dick Ciccone and John Sevcik.

CONTENTS

Acknowledgments xi
Foreword xiii
Introduction 1

PART I: NEWS THAT WASN'T BREAKING

The Angel Of West Madison Street 7
Jim Crow At The Abraham Lincoln Hotel 11
Death Of A President 17
Niagara 23
Twin Brothers 27
A Missing Woman 33
Two Cops Dead 35
An Oral History 39
A Prisoner Of War 43
The Hunters 45
Breakdown 47
The Election 51
The Fetcher 53
Miflin Street 57
Providence St. Mel 61
Chicago Housing Authority 65

The Fisherman 71

Inheritance 75

A Tip From The FBI 79

Justice 83

Stateville Prison Riot... 85

City Savings And Loan 89

Sludge: Chicago's Liquid Gold 93

The Mayor Of Rosemont 99

PART II: THE CHARACTERS

Andy Mcgann 109

A Model Inmate... 113

Bobby Rush 117

"Bull Jive".. 121

Epton Before It's Too Late... 123

Otto Kerner 131

Hoffa.. 137

Lunch With Sid Luckman 141

Crossing The Rhine... 145

Chick Mccuen 149

Pat Boyle 155

PART III: TINY TALES

Live Television 161

St. Gabe's... 165

Forgiveness.. 169

Snow News 171

The President In Town... 175

Back Pay.. 181

That Nice Little Lady At The Loan Company........................ 183
How Geraldo Scooped Me 185

PART IV: THE COMMENTATOR

They Buried Jimmy Nolan.. 189
New Mayor Takes Bodyguards From The Old Mayor........... 191
Driving The Kids To Florida 193
An Economic Story.. 195
Health Scare On Scotch 197
Nasty Politics... 199
Ted Kennedy And Roger Mudd 201
Roland Burris... 203
Wasteful Bureaucracy 205
The Eighteen Wheeler Behind You 207
None Of The Above.. 209
Back To School... 211

About the Author 213
About the Back Cover... 215
Photo Section.. 217
Index 239

ACKNOWLEDGMENTS

I want to thank Rob Price and Tony Cellini for their fine work in getting this book published. Many thanks to Bob Boone of Young Chicago Authors for writing the Foreword. Over the years I worked with many wonderfully talented people, news managers, producers, writers, reporters camera crews, engineers, at WMAQ and WBBM-TV, too many too mention here. I thank them all. Some of my friends and colleagues were generous with their advice during the writing of this book: Joe Howard, Jim Strong, Mike Houlihan, Bill Cameron, the veteran city hall reporter, Jim Stricklin and Dick Kay. Thanks to Bill Crawford for his time and advice. Gratitude to Alderman Ed Burke of the Chicago City Council and his assistant, Donal Quinlan for providing archival material. Thanks to Joe Winston of Sawgrass Productions for his technical help with photos. M.J. Keller helped as my assistant during the final months of this project. My son, Stephen, read the manuscript and offered advice. Patrick and Matt Nolan and Anna Mazzucchelli were always available to answer my cyber questions. So was Monte Parker my El Conquistador neighbor. Thanks to Tine Mazz, Mary Nolan and Cara Lanscioni for their encouragement. Special thanks to staff members of the Newberry, and Glenview libraries who were always so helpful during my research. Chicago's Harold Washington Library has an excellent Municipal Reference Section. Two staff members there, Sarah Erekson and Morag Walsh, were of great help on this project. Thanks to Stephen Seddon for the index.

—Peter Nolan

FOREWORD

Peter Nolan may have been a no nonsense reporter in a no-nonsense city, but at heart he was a great storyteller. He knows how to start a story, develop it and bring it to a close. He knows how to put in the right detail at the right time. He writes in a clear, simple, caring way. He's there next to you sharing something important.

Like all great storytellers, Peter takes us to fascinating places. This might be the field outside of Altgeld Gardens where the local kids hunt rabbits. A street in Madison Wisconsin in the early 70's, with traces of tear gas lingering after a night of anti war riots. A courtroom with the lawyer and his client—a severe stutterer—singing to each other. A school on the west side fighting for survival. A battlefield in Europe at the end of WW II.

Peter fills his stories with fascinating people. Some we know already—Jimmy Hoffa, Otto Kerner, JFK's sister, Bernie Epton. But while these are familiar he finds something new to say about them. (One of his pieces is called "Lunch with Sid Luckman") Mostly Peter's people are not so well known at all, but they should be. The Angel of West Madison Street, the Fetcher, the fisherman, the model prisoner.

He has picked his stories for a reason. Some exhibit quiet

heroism. Some show Chicago at its most typical. Other stories are utterly surprising.

Some add to our understanding; others make us question what we thought we knew.

This book should reach a lot of people: the serious Chicago scholar looking for more particulars, the weekend scholar satisfying his curiosity, a student of human nature, or just someone looking for a good story.

Whoever you are, you are going to enjoy this book. When you've finished, put it on the shelf next to books by Mike Royko and Ben Hecht.

—Bob Boone,
author, founder Young Chicago Authors

INTRODUCTION

WHEN I LEFT television news for good in 1986 I brought with me the scripts I had written over the years in Chicago and I put them in boxes. And I put them up in the attic where they rested until I moved to another, smaller house after all our kids had left home.

The scripts came with me and they were placed up in the rafters of our attached garage because there was no attic in the new house. There they remained for another nine or so years until I brought them down and began to sort through them.

I even bought some loose leaf folders and one of those punch hole gadgets and arranged the scripts in these folders according to date.

For awhile I wasn't sure why I was doing this. I think I wanted to have them for my children and my grandchildren. Probably I wanted to let them know Papa was a broadcast journalist during a very interesting period of the twentieth century, the 60's, 70's and 80's.

I worked in Television News in its infancy. And I was there many years later when it probably began its decline. I was at a television station in the mid 1960's when the entire staff gathered in a studio. The owner pulled a switch and the audience watched their picture go from black and white to full color. We went from film to video tape. In the early days women at the stations where I worked had jobs as secretaries, book keepers, and receptionists. At WKBN TV in Youngstown, Ohio, there was one woman in our newsroom, Doris Saloom, the secretary. In my mind she was capable of running the place but her title was newsroom secretary. When I came to Chicago in 1968 I was writing for a pioneering woman anchor, Jorie Lueloff. When I wrote on the midnight newscast my boss was a young female producer, Lucyna Migala. Valetta Press, secretary to the famous old commentator, Len O'Connor, was promoted to network field producer. Women took on jobs as camera operators and sound technicians. By the time I was through, women may have outnumbered the men. People of color started coming to work in our newsroom. NBC was a leader in this effort. It was good.

I don't pretend to be that important. I was in the business before radio and television news people had gained the celebrity status they have today, although the transition was definitely beginning in the eighties. The biggest, most visible job I ever had was delivering a nightly commentary on the ten o'clock news on Channel 5 (NBC) in Chicago from 1978 to 1981. I've included some of those commentaries in one of the chapters. It's funny as so many years pass, the old issues become the new issues. I remember when I was in Niagara Falls, New York in 1963, one of the big issues was something called railroad relocation. Like so many American towns and cities automobiles were being delayed by trains crossing main roads. One of our listeners sent me a clipping from and old Niagara Fall Gazette in the early 1900's. The banner headline read: City Council to tackle railroad relocation.

Most of the stories in this book were broadcast at one time or another. The few that were not were stories I came upon that I found compelling. My hope is that you, the reader, will have the same impression.

About a half century ago someone in the newsroom at WMAQ-TV Chicago clipped a cartoon from the New Yorker and posted it on the bulletin board, It showed a man standing in front of a closed. door He's confronted by a TV reporter with microphone and camera. "You'll never believe what's happening in this room," the man exclaims. "Tell me about it says the reporter."

Television today has become radio. You can see the people talking away in the studio but that's all. Analysis masquerades as the real thing.

—Peter Nolan
Glenview, IL
January, 2018

PART I

NEWS THAT WASN'T BREAKING

THE ANGEL OF WEST MADISON STREET

Circa 1987

O N ONE OF the steel girders holding up the elevated tracks there was a small stenciled number. It was number thirty-one. Perhaps it was an identification number of some sort, of interest to engineers or maintenance people from the Chicago Transit Authority.

Yet the businessman, standing there under the elevated tracks with the priest made a great fuss over it. "Isn't that incredible," he said, pointing up at it. "It was thirty-one years ago that I met you, Monsignor. On this very spot. Thirty-one years ago this month." "The good Lord has his signs," said the priest. The businessman wore an expensive summer suit. He was stocky with a round Irish face. The priest was bigger and older. He had a ruddy face and a shock of white hair. The priest was Monsignor Ignatius McDermott, the pastor of skid row, the padre of West Madison Street in Chicago. A man, who for forty years, ministered to the drunks and the down and outers. He picked them up from the dirt and gave them a bowl of soup and a clean place to sleep. He had roamed the streets at night for forty years. Sometimes he protected them from jack rollers and sometimes he just stopped to visit in their bars or their chicken-wired flop houses. When they went to the hospital to have their diseased limbs amputated he went to see them. Always he urged them toward sobriety. Few of them ever escaped the confines of skid row. Oh, there might be a brief foraging expedition to North Clark Street or Uptown. Once in awhile someone might drift to another city and another bottle gang and was never heard from again. But most of them never got out. This was the end of the line until they put them in a box. Father Mac gave them a funeral service too, and a decent burial. But this man, the businessman standing under the el tracks with Monsignor McDermott, was different. He had become a millionaire in real estate, billboards and chain restaurants. The road had ended here at Van Buren and Lasalle Streets thirty-one years ago. And it also had begun.

He grew up in New York City, East Harlem, the same neighborhood where Jimmy Cagney grew up. They were poor. The family moved from one cold water flat to another.

As soon as he was old enough he learned how to hustle money along Third Avenue. He sold day old flowers and recovered copper wire from vacant buildings, selling it to junk dealers. And he had a job cleaning out the vats at some cider stands. That's where he took his first drink. When he was cleaning out the vats in the morning he would drink the hard cider and then go off to grammar school with a buzz on.

Before long drinking became the most important thing in his life. He worked only to get money for booze. He drifted from job to job. Life became a blur of alcoholic binges and bar room fights. All the while his Irish mother said rosaries for him. He even stole money from her to get a drink. His encounters with the law were getting serious, grand larceny, assault, robbery. One day he found himself in front of a judge who was threatening to send him to jail. He swore on the bible that he'd never take another drink in his life and somehow the judge gave him a pass. Still, he didn't stop drinking. His health deteriorated. He was throwing up blood. Only then did he decide to quit. He got help and he stopped drinking. He stayed sober for three and a half months.

Some friends got him a job offer with a major firm in Chicago and he went there to start a new life. The year was 1955. He took up residence in a North side apartment with four other alcoholics The businessman recalled all of this when he came back to visit Father Mac, more than thirty years later.

"I had worked at the new job only three days. One day one of my roommates came home with a bottle of bourbon and it was all over. I drifted to skid row and stayed in flop houses. The binge went on for about thirty days. Even the worst alcoholic must take a pause from drinking to let his body rest. It was during one of these periods that I decided to end it. I was twenty-three years old and my life was over. There's a quiet resignation that takes place when you're gonna knock yourself off. I remember I had been in a fight and I must have been kicked in the head. For a number of days this stuff kept draining from my ear. It looked like black coffee. I went across the street under the el tracks to Pixley and Ellers to get a cup of coffee but mainly to get napkins to stop this stuff from coming out of my ear. As I left the flop house it was about eleven o'clock at night. There was no one on the street. That's when I saw him for the first time. Eleven o'clock at night in a tough neighborhood and here's this Catholic priest. I asked him if he knew where I could get my ear fixed. It's funny when you think back on it. Here I'm about to kill myself, go out the window of my hotel, and I want to get my ear fixed.

The priest talked to me and he expressed a concern for me. I really can't remember his exact words, but I know he directed me to a hospital somewhere up on the North side. I went up there on the elevated and they treated my ear. The next morning

I woke up and there was a quiet peace in my room. There wasn't any booze in the room because I couldn't afford any. But booze wasn't the first thing on my mind and I realized I had lost the compulsion to drink. I haven't had a drink since, not even a thimble-full of beer."

Later he went to Holy Cross Mission where he saw Monsignor McDermott again. He got food and clothing and later he found work. He met a girl and they got married and raised a family. He went into business and became a huge success.

Now, as he reminisced about that chance meeting that changed his life so many years ago, the businessman said: "Somewhere in the Bible they talk of people who come into your lives who are angels, God's anointed ones. And they are sent for a reason. When I think of this particular passage I think of Father Mac."

JIM CROW AT THE ABRAHAM LINCOLN HOTEL

Circa 1975

THE DEACON WALKED up the open stairway slowly. He was heavy set and past the age of seventy-five. So it took some time for him to reach the top. His companions, three younger men, waited below. It was a white house, or was it a house? It could have been a restaurant at one time. It was a ramshackle affair. And it seemed as though many extensions to the original building had been added on over the years. But it was hard to tell because the place was partially hidden by an overgrowth of brush and scrap trees like the hearty trees of heaven. There was an entrance on the ground floor too and a small old broken canopy leading to it. But this hadn't been used for a long time because it too was overgrown with brush. What looked like an old piece of a neon sign hung from one side of the canopy. The Deacon paused for a moment at the top of the stairs and smiled an old private smile as he rang the door bell. In a few seconds a woman's voice penetrated the warm air of this late Spring day. It seemed to startle the Deacon until he realized it came from an intercom box by the side of the door.

But the sound of the voice was very clear and real. It seemed that it came from the trees:

"Who's there. Is somebody out there?"

"Is that you Rosalie?"

"Who is it?"

"Why it's Deacon Davis, Rosalie."

"Oh my Lord, Deacon. I'm an invalid now. I can't get out of bed. And my girl went into town, so I can't open the door. But oh my Lord, is it you, Reverend?"

"That's OK honey. You just stay where you are. But I had some fellas here with me and I was telling them what it was like in the old days. I was telling them we were here every night, practically every night."

"Yes, that's right honey."

"And I was telling them some of the greats that were here."

"Yes, yes."

"You know what I wanted, I wanted them to see all the pictures of Louie Armstrong and Cab Calloway and all that crowd that used to come here."

"Oh yes."

"Well, you take care now dear."

It was 1975 and Corneal A. Davis was in his thirty-third year as a member of the Illinois General Assembly on the day he took us over by Rosalie's place, or what was left of it. He was the grandson of slaves and had come up to Chicago from Mississippi. Deacon was a real title, not a nickname. He had been educated at the Moody Bible Institute and was an assistant pastor of the A.M.E. Church. He was often called upon to give the prayer when the Illinois House began its sessions. The Deacon also had a law degree from the John Marshall School of Law in Chicago. He had been in World War I in combat as a stretcher bearer and later served with the Eighth Infantry, Illinois National Guard. He would laugh as he told the story of being in the trenches in France. "We had a young Captain who shouted every time he led the men on a charge: 'Up men, for Lafayette, for Lafayette!' Hell, I didn't even know who Lafayette was." The Deacon ended up in politics in Chicago's second ward on the South side, part of Congressman Bill Dawson's organization. Corneal Davis was known as the Dean of the Illinois House because no other member had served longer at that time. He was an assistant majority leader. He had been through all of the civil rights battles and been a champion of fair employment and fair housing legislation. On this day he was giving a speech in support of the equal rights amendment for women. His gravelly, baritone voice thundered into the microphone but it seemed that no one was paying attention. The Illinois House had one hundred and seventy-seven members in those days and people were milling all about. Some were eating fried chicken and pizza at their desks. Others were gathered in little caucuses in the aisles. It was difficult to hear anything in this raucous atmosphere. One of those who walked by, seemingly oblivious to Representative Davis, was Representative Harold Washington, who would later become a U.S. Congressman and the first black mayor of Chicago. That's how it was in the Illinois House in those days. But the Deacon rolled on.

"When I first came to Springfield, this is the reception I got, being ignored. I slept in the GM&O with Senator C.C. Wimbish. I slept in the train station over there. You're talking about equal rights and I think I should say it. There wasn't a place downtown where I could get a sandwich. I was a minister and I rented a room at Rosalie's on the East side. Now, I don't think what I'm going to say is important, but I have the same right as any man in here to speak. And I fought for that right for every black person in here. And I'll fight again for them, the right to have this floor." The next day Deacon Davis and I took a walk through downtown Springfield. We visited the old GM & O station where he first arrived in 1942 and then went over to the Abraham Lincoln Hotel. The building was vacant and boarded up on the ground floor, though we were able to peek through some broken glass here and there. Later we sat in the warm sun between the Centennial Building and the Capitol and Representative Davis reminisced some more. "What I like most now," he said, "is being able to say what's on your mind, without fear of someone putting a shotgun to your head. " But it wasn't that way when he arrived in Springfield in 1942. He wasn't sure where he could stay. His friend, Senator C.C. Wimbish, assured him that he had been promised accommodations at the Abraham Lincoln Hotel.

"And so we went up to the Abraham Lincoln Hotel with our confirmation in hand, and we got in line, Wimbish in front and me in back. When he walked up to sign in, the man pulled the book away and he said: 'You boys don't live here in Springfield do you? Because, if you did, you'd know better than to come and try to register in a hotel in Springfield, Illinois.' Everything in me seemed to drop out of me. I said, uh oh, this is it! Wimbish tried to explain the law to him. And so the man came out from behind the desk and he says, 'I don't care what the law is. And I don't care if you are lawyers. Before I let any niggers stay in this hotel I'll close it up.' I says to him, I don't know if I'll ever pass any laws in this town, but I'll tell you what I'm gonna do. I'm gonna dedicate my whole life in Springfield to help you realize your ambition and that is to close up this hotel."

Corneal Davis lived to be over ninety years of age before he died. When he retired from the legislature he went back to Chicago and was appointed a commissioner of the city's board of elections by Harold Washington. He served in that position for several years in the 1980's. Many years after he had left Springfield and the Illinois General Assembly they tore down the Abraham Lincoln Hotel and Corneal Davis went back down to see it. He stood there on the sidewalk and watched. Someone took a picture of the Deacon looking on as the wrecking ball did its work. The photo made one of the news wires and was printed in newspapers around the state.

DEATH of a PRESIDENT

1963

I GOT MY FIRST *job in radio at WHLD Niagara Falls in July of 1963. Our studios were in the Parkway Inn, a nice tourist hotel on the river just upstream from the Falls. Our station broadcast the Yankee games with Mel Allen calling the play by play. There was a lot of excitement at the station that summer. A popular TV series called Route 66 was filming an episode in Niagara Falls. It starred Martin Milner and George Maharis as two young dudes roaming the country in a Corvette and finding themselves in the middle of interesting stories. Some of the staff signed up as extras and took vacation time to do it. Most were disappointed when they had to sit for hours before uttering their only line and getting paid fifty dollars. There was a night bellhop at the hotel who used to bring me coffee early in the morning and I let him look at the sports scores on our news wire. I think he was a gambler. He relished telling me what time the young Route 66 stars got back to the hotel in the morning. The Route 66 crew finally wrapped up and went on its way. The episode was about the assassination of a foreign potentate visiting Niagara Falls. The show was scheduled for a November airing but it had to be cancelled.*

I was in college during the 1960 Presidential campaign,

an upper classman at Villanova. My friends and I were all thrilled at the prospects of young Senator Jack Kennedy of Massachusetts. He was a handsome, dashing guy, a World War II Naval combat veteran. He was a lot like us, Irish and Catholic. But that's where the similarity ended. Jack Kennedy was rich beyond anything we might know. His father had been a banker, a Wall Street financier and a Hollywood B-movie maker. When the stock market crashed Joe Kennedy was out of it. He had sold all his holdings and was heavy with cash. During the depression he went down to Palm Beach Florida and began buying up prime real estate at dirt cheap prices. One of them was Chicago's Merchandise Mart, the largest building in the world in square feet then. Several years later I would go to work there as an NBC News writer on the nineteenth floor.

Joe Kennedy also had a tip that prohibition was about to end. So he went to England, signed up some big distillers and became the exclusive U.S. distributer for some brand name whiskey, gin and other spirits. Life was good for the Kennedy's.

In late September of 1960 we were in our dorms glued to the TV watching Senator Jack debate Vice President Richard Nixon. Nixon was the front runner in the campaign. We all thought Kennedy whipped him that night in Chicago. The next day the print media saw the debate as a draw. Most of the newspapers in those days were Republican.

That debate helped John F. Kennedy squeeze out a narrow victory on election day, making him the thirty-fifth president of the United States. It was Camelot for awhile. Jackie Kennedy was stunningly beautiful. The couple had a darling little girl and Mrs Kennedy was expecting another child. The President spoke to the people of Berlin in German. Jackie spoke a little French in public.

I graduated from Villanova, promptly got married, had a

short stint as a teacher, then got hired as a newsman in Niagara Falls.

In July we welcomed our first child, a baby girl named Christine.

My radio station had an eclectic programming schedule; Music and news during morning and afternoon drive time. After 9AM came the religious shows with names like Back to the Bible, Brother Billy, and the Hebrew/Christian hour with Dr. Michaelson who had been converted from Judaism to Christianity. I sometimes had to field phone calls from irate listeners who wondered what that was all about. We also had foreign language shows including a Ukrainian hour where the host constantly attacked the Communist regime in his homeland. The station had a daytime license and we went off the air at sundown.

Another program was the Christian Century Hour with Rev. Carl McIntire, a conservative, Evangelical preacher. Rev. McIntire broadcast every day from his own hotel, The Christian Admiral in Cape May, New Jersey. He had no use for President John F. Kennedy and, as I prepared my newscast each day I could hear the on air speaker and the good Reverend railing against the President. There were others who didn't like Kennedy who had far more evil intent.

As a young newsman my schedule was all over the board: police and fire beats at the crack of dawn, phone calls to other news places, morning newscasts, city hall, criminal courts, afternoon newscasts, sometimes school board and city council meetings at night.

On Friday, November 22nd I finished a five minute newscast at 12:30 PM and drove to my home about fifteen minutes away. I had something to eat and headed to my bed for a nap. It seemed like a quiet day and I didn't have to be back at the station until 2:30 PM. I must have dozed off because the ringing of the phone awoke me. And then my wife's voice calling from the kitchen. Peter, you have to go the the station right away. Somebody shot President Kennedy in Dallas.

My boss, the station manager Eddy Joseph, was waiting at the door to the studio when I got there. He had a roll of wire copy in his hand. Go in and start reading. We'll feed you the copy. Your the news director. This is what we pay you for.

I was on the job for only five months and still a little nervous in front of a live mike.

They were bulletins at first. The President had been shot in an open convertible as he motorcaded through Dallas. He had been taken to Parkland Memorial Hospital.

In those days the wire services put a label on many stories. The least important was "urgent", much like the label we see so much of today on television as breaking news, or news alert. This can be anything that just came into the newsroom. More important was a story sent as a bulletin. I was reading many bulletins that afternoon on WHLD in Niagara Falls as the story of the shooting of the President unfolded from Dallas.

And then came what I had never seen before on the wire. FLASH! President John F. Kennedy is dead. I would later learn that the designation FLASH was reserved for monumental stories such as the end of a World War or the assassination of a head of state.

I kept reading what came over the wire that afternoon. Then there was a nice break. The Mayor of Niagara Falls, E. Dent Lackey, was in the hotel. Lackey was a flamboyant character who sometimes rode a white horse in parades. White haired, mustached, he was a great orator. He was also a Presbyterian minister. He was interviewed for a long time by my boss, Eddy Joseph. It gave me a chance to gather my wits and continue my work until sunset when we went off the air. Sundown was early that Friday in November.

I came to work early the next morning. My friend, the hotel bellhop, showed up with hot coffee as usual. As I entered our main studio I was stunned to see the boxes, where I had put all the historic wire copy and newspapers were gone. "Oh my God!" The bellhop said a cleaning person had just taken them away. He rushed out to see if he could catch him. When he came back he said it was too late the stuff had gone in the incinerator.

I remember we played a lot of sacred music that day interspersed with reports from me on what was happening in Dallas and Washington and in Niagara Falls, the announcements from Churches, temples and other institutions that were having memorial services for President Kennedy. Later that day Mr. Joseph announced he had made arrangements for us to join the Mutual radio network for the next few days including the funeral of President Kennedy.

I went home and watched the rest of the story unfold on Television. All of those pictures, President Lyndon Johnson taking the oath of office on Air Force One as Mrs. Kennedy looks on, the eulogies, that beautiful poem by Senator Mike Mansfield, "She took a ring from her finger and placed it in his hand," John John saluting the casket, the riderless horse and the drumbeat.

My wife and I took turns going to Church on Sunday while the other watched our baby. I can still see her shouting from our upper porch as I walked toward our house. "Hurry up, you've got to see this on television." A guy named Jack Ruby, a strip club owner had just shot Lee Harvey Oswald, alleged assassin of the president.

I still have Jack Kennedy's Mass card. On the front is a formal portrait of the young President with a sad hint of a smile. On the back is a prayer asking for the forgiveness of all his sins.

NIAGARA

Circa 1965

*I*N THE NEWS *business Niagara Falls was what they called a glamorous dateline. Site of one of the world's great wonders, it also had a romantic aspect. Newspaper, news wire and broadcast editors were always interested. Maybe it was some nut going over the Falls in a barrel, or a photo of tourists on the Maid of the Mist going underneath the Falls. Or maybe it was some despondent businessman who came five hundred miles from New York City to do the Dutch act in style. The usual procedure was to leave the wallet, shoes and socks on shore, then wade into the rapids from Goat Island. The body would wash up down river in Lake Ontario a few days later. I once reported a story about Niagara Falls that would rock the nation and the world. It forecast the demise of the Falls.*

I was the news director of WHLD radio, a five thousand watt AM-FM station that covered all of Western New York and a good chunk of Southern Ontario Including Toronto. I had the title of news director but the only person I directed was myself. I was the only news person. The station manager was big on local news. So I got up every day at 5 AM, went to the police and fire headquarters, city hall, the courts and any other place where news might be happening. I made phone calls to

other news sources. I wrote and delivered five newscasts a day
and wrote headlines for disc jockeys and announcers to read
at other times during the day. I mimeographed a daily news
letter and drove it around to restaurants and clubs. Sometimes
there were city council and school board meetings at night. I
covered those too. There was a break of nearly two hours in
the afternoon when I could get a bite to eat and sometimes
a nap. The pay was one hundred and five dollars a week
and I loved it. I had a darling wife and two cute little girls
home in an upper flat on 24th Street. I didn't know it then
but, thinking back, it was as close to heaven as you can get.
As the song so aptly says: That was once upon a time very long
ago.

I worked until noon on Saturday and was off on Sunday
when the station broadcast religious programs. Once my boss
asked me to work on Sunday to carry out a very important
assignment. The Niagara Falls Gazette was going to break a
blockbuster story in its Sunday edition. He wasn't even informed
as to the content of the story but he thought it had something
to do with the Geology of Niagara Falls. My job was to go in
that Sunday, read the newspaper story and then write a shorter
version for broadcast. I was to break into programming with
the first bulletin, then provide written copy for the announcers
for the rest of the day.

I was stunned when I got to the station and saw the Sunday
Gazette. The front page screamed with ink. I hadn't seen that
much ink on a front page since President John F. Kennedy
was assassinated a couple of years earlier. The American Falls
was crumbling. It could disintegrate into a series of cascades.
Erosion over time had moved the cataract back from its original
position. Now the whole thing might crumble.

As I carefully read through this long story, one thing kept
nagging at me. There were no named sources. It was always:

Geologists say. Engineers and experts fear. Those who did have their names in the story were the politicians, local and national. Of course they were very worried and concerned about the fate of Niagara Falls and pledged to do something about it. In those days the newspapers were very powerful and the politicians were always anxious to do their bidding. Today the power lies with the cable TV talk shows.

I called my boss and expressed my concern about the absence of named sources. He told me to forget about it, just attribute everything to the newspaper. We didn't want to make an enemy of the Niagara Falls Gazette.

And so it was. The story of the great demise of the American Falls was ongoing. Congressional inquiries began. Studies were made by the U.S. Army Corps of Engineers. Commissions were formed. It took a long time but the story eventually faded from the world and national news and the front pages of papers. But the Niagara Falls Gazette was relentless.

In 1966 I got a job in television. I went to WKBN in Youngstown, Ohio and learned how to do news stories with black and white optical film. While I was there the station began broadcasting in color. A couple of new kids arrived in our family. Niagara Falls faded from memory..

In 1968 I took a job as a summer replacement writer at NBC News in Chicago. In the Fall of that year I became a permanent employee.

One day in 1969 I was in the 19th floor NBC newsroom in the Merchandise Mart. I noticed with great interest a story that moved on one of the wire services. The U.S. Army Corps of Engineers was shutting down the American Falls of Niagara. A coffer dam was to be built to divert water from the river away from that part of the Falls. Then test borings would be made to see if something could be done to prevent future rock slides and erosion. I went to my bosses and volunteered to go and cover the story. I had first hand knowledge. But they said no. Let New York worry about it.

And they did build the dam and shut down the Falls for a time and the test borings were made. And then the Falls resumed flowing. And the American Falls is still working today. Maybe the predictions of disintegration will come true someday but it might take a couple of thousand years.

It was one hell of a story at the time. I'm sure it will be revived by some enterprising editor some day. "Do you remember the time they shut down Niagara Falls?"

Twin Brothers

Circa 1985

Bob Casey was a prominent attorney in St. Charles, Illinois, a far Western suburb of Chicago. Casey had represented that area in the Illinois General Assembly in the late 50's and early 1960's. He retired from politics and returned to his law practice. But he remained active in political circles and that's where I met him in my work as a political reporter.

Casey was a capable lawyer, an agreeable, popular guy. Silver haired and silver tongued, he could smooth over very difficult situations. He never ran for public office again, but because of his talents, in 1988 the Republican Party of Kane County asked him to serve as state's attorney when there was a vacancy in that office. Casey was to fill an unexpired term while the party decided on a permanent replacement.

Casey, himself, would say later that his experience in criminal law was very limited. But the office had an experienced and gifted head of the criminal division, John Barsanti. Casey and Barsanti would encounter the biggest murder case in the history of the county.

This is the treatment of a screenplay Casey asked me to write when it was all over and it pretty well sums up the story.

*   *   *

It is June 1987. The scene is an offbeat tavern called Bandito Barney's in the far western Chicago suburb of East Dundee near Carpentersville. It's a town where the urban sprawl meets the country. There are about seventy-five people in the tavern. A toast is being made to a young man who is seated at the bar dressed in a baseball uniform. Upon closer inspection it becomes apparent that this young man is not alive. His eyes stare straight ahead into the mirror behind the bar. There is a bullet wound on the side of his head. A drink is in front of him. Friends on either side prop him up. Suddenly someone shouts: "Oh my God, he's starting to leak!" There's a rush to grab the body, some tables are shoved together, and the young man is gently lowered down. He lies in state as the party continues.

The next day in bright sunlight we see the body again propped up in the seat of a 1966 Corvette. The dead man's twin brother is at the wheel. They drive through town in a journey of farewell. Friends follow in a motorcade. There is frequent honking of horns and people waving from the street. Two gorgeous young women sob uncontrollably from the sidewalk as they recognize the handsome young dead man. Finally the motorcade comes to a stop in a small park where a makeshift funeral service is conducted. Speeches and final tributes are made to the deceased who still sits in the front seat of the Corvette. The twin brother pleads with the undertaker to have his sibling buried in the Corvette but the undertaker tells him that's impossible.

The dead man is thirty-five year old Tim McNamee, a flamboyant young attorney with a taste for fast cars and faster women. Everyone in town knows Tim, especially the young girls he left in his wake, some of them bitter about the way he treated them. The cops knew Tim too. He made many of them look like fools in the courtroom as he exposed their bungling ways and got many of his clients off. Because of Tim McNamee a lot of local drug dealers walked. The cops knew this well and some of them even threatened to get Tim.

Who killed Tim McNamee? A jilted lover? A disgruntled drug dealer? Was he set up by some angry cops? Was Tim himself involved with drugs? Or was it someone else?

The McNamees were a large family of stunningly attractive children who, despite a tough childhood, managed to become overachievers. Many of the McNamee kids stayed in Carpentersville and lived in a rambling log cabin called the "ranch," a place where they partied with their friends.Tim and his twin brother Thom often wore green tuxedos at St. Patrick's Day celebrations. Thom also was an attorney, a male model and would-be actor. Thom didn't trust the cops and took it upon himself to solve his brother's murder with the help of private investigators.

Flashback to the night of June 7, 1987. The scene is a small ranch house converted to an office building and located just off a busy highway. The building houses the law offices of Tim Mahoney and Tim McNamee. Both men are the same age, height, weight and general physical description. Both drive the same style car, a late model black Porsche. McNamee's car is parked in Mahoney's space this particular evening. At about 10 PM, his work finished, Tim McNamee steps out into the parking lot. A shadowy figure, lurking in a nearby grove of trees, raises an old rifle to his shoulder. There is one loud report and Tim McNamee slumps to the ground. Within seconds a car screeches to a halt on the road, there's a sound of running footsteps, a door slamming and the car speeding away.

The investigation of the McNamee case was going nowhere. Thom McNamee, a young man with a hot temper, was leery of the police. And he was enraged that police were dropping hints in the media that his brother had a drug connection. Thom needed money to finance his own private investigation. So he staged a fabulous fund raising party at Chicago's Field Museum of Natural History. All the beautiful people of Chicago's "eighties" culture were there, including several Chicago Bear stars, actors and actresses.

Police finally zeroed in on a woman named Nadine Walter. Nadine was well known to the cops and the local media. She was a loud, loose-tongued, loose-hipped woman who frequently held news conferences charging that the police weren't doing enough to find her son. The three year old boy was believed to have been kidnapped by Nadine's ex husband, Rolando. Nadine had a pretty good motive too. The ex husband had been represented in a bitter custody battle by none other than Tim Mahoney, Tim McNamee's law partner. It was well known that Nadine hated Mahoney. Nadine also had a new boyfriend, Bill Nally. Nally was one of the nastiest men in the far Western suburbs, a former outlaw biker, ex con and enforcer for local drug dealers. Everybody knew he was mean enough to do it.

The big break came when Nadine got jammed up in a stolen credit card scheme. A convicted felon, arrested by police, told them that Nadine had gone with him on several charging sprees. An ex con herself, Nadine was looking at some heavy jail time. Detectives put on the squeeze. They arrested her and then put her in a hotel where lawyers offered her a deal; immunity on the murder charge and credit card scam if she would give them Bill Nally in return. It was a wild few days in the hotel. Nadine refused to eat. Then she tried to seduce several officers if they'd let her go. Finally Nadine agreed to tell her story. But there was one small problem. Nadine was a notorious liar. She had admitted lying to the grand jury. Would a jury believe her story? The lawyers decided they needed more evidence. They needed Bill Nally on tape.

The dramatic conclusion to the story takes place at O'Hare International Airport. Nally is due to to arrive on a plane from Utah. Nadine is wired for sound. Undercover police are all over the place, listening to their radios, poised to move in if she can get him to say it.

* * *

Nadine met Bill Nally as he exited a plane from Utah. She was wearing a wire and the State Police could hear her conversation with him. Nadine seems panicked. She keeps telling Bill the police are following her. What should she do if they offer her immunity. Nally is cool. He says they're just trying to scare her. If they stick by their story that they were out of town at the time of the murder it will be ok.. They argue about the old rifle, the murder weapon. Nadine wants to know if it's traceable. But finally Nadine gets Nally to say: I went and got a gun in the morning and I killed the motherfucker. I killed the motherfucker the same day.

* * *

The tape helped John Barsanti successfully prosecute William Nally. He was found guilty and sentenced to life in prison where he died in 2007.

Some years later Bob Casey asked if he could hire me to write the story. He knew I dabbled in writing and had written a play. Casey said he had been out in California and met an executive with one of the major Hollywood talent agencies who was very interested in the McNamee murder case. He asked Bob to provide some material and that's why he thought of me.

Having had a couple of brushes with Hollywood I told Bob Casey I would be happy to provide a synopsis of the story which he could submit to his agent friend. If the story sold they could pay me a standard fee. I was given access to the state's attorney's files, court transcripts and had a long interview with John Barsanti. Time passed and nothing ever happened in Hollywood.

Nadine Walter disappeared into the witness protection program. She would reappear years later in Florida where she had changed her life. Under an assumed name she was happily married with three children. In 2006 she had a law degree from Florida A&M University and passed the state bar exam. She was working in a state's attorney's office when someone there got wind of her record. Thom McNamee got word of this too and he asked that she be denied admission to the bar. Nadine resigned from her position in the state's attorney's office and disappeared again into the witness protection program and hasn't been heard from since.

Thom McNamee went back to his many business interests in Carpenersville, IL. He liked to tool around in his pickup truck sporting Wyoming license plates which said rebl. He died of brain cancer in 2009 at the age of fifty-six.

Bob Casey, the former state's attorney for Kane County died in 2006. He was eighty-five.

A MISSING WOMAN

Circa 1974

THE WEATHER WAS brilliant on this particular Sunday in October. It was Chicago but it looked more like San Diego. Blue skies, 70's, the boats, still in the harbors, awaiting winter storage or voyages South to warmer places. Thousands of people strolled along Michigan Avenue.

At the Hilton Hotel the Governor was scheduled to speak.

On Madison Street the mass was just ending at St. Peter's Church and worshipers were lingering outside. For one woman it was a bit of a reunion. Her family had lived in Chicago for several years when her husband was a public official. But they had since returned to the East. She still had friends here.

Yet, this woman returned to Chicago periodically, to visit her sister who was confined to a special home run by the sisters in Wisconsin. She would pick her sister up and then come to Chicago where they would stay in a downtown hotel.

The sister, who was in her mid fifties, had never really been right from the beginning. As a child she couldn't keep up with her siblings in this large competitive family. The father saw what was happening. He tried to correct it. In the end there was electric shock treatment, a common practice at that time. That made things worse and she came gradually to another place where there was no time and space. Perhaps she could see her brothers or a sister who had died so young.

At the church the crowd was thinning. And a sudden wave of fear came over the other sister when she lost sight of the afflicted one. She went inside the church, then quickly out on the street again. She called for help and police arrived immediately.

A woman, of medium height and weight had wondered off. She was wearing a white blazer and red flannel slacks. She was unable to communicate or take care of her basic needs. If she walked East, toward the lake, she would probably be alright. But if she walked West and crossed the river, there was danger.

A reporter commented to a colleague: "When Mayor Daley finds out who it is, the police will be everywhere. And so they were. But there was no sign of the missing woman. And, as the time passed, the possibility of another Kennedy family tragedy loomed.

A reporter, who knew what was happening, saw her walking slowly on Michigan Avenue across from the Art Institute. It was determined many years later that she had walked into Orchestra Hall. Attendants let her take a seat in the rear. The performance was almost over and the woman was " dressed so nice."

On the street the reporter approached her. The family resemblance was unmistakeable. "Are you looking for your sister?" But there was no answer, just a far away look, another time and place. From a distance, a cameraman recorded the scene. "Are you looking for Eunice?" There was just the slightest hint of recollection in her eyes. "Call the police", the reporter shouted. Two way radios were engaged. Within moments the police arrived and the woman was taken back to her sister.

Her brother, the senator, would send a letter of thanks .There was no family tragedy this time.

Those would remain in the past. Others would await their own time and place. Her name was Rosemary.

Two Cops Dead

Circa 1974

"COPS USE EXCESSIVE *force out of fear. That's always the case. They get in trouble when that fear is unfounded. But they don't know if it's real or not. They're driven by fear." (interview with a Chicago policeman.)*

"I can't believe it. He was sitting right next to me. We decided to throw some darts. It happened so fast. I mean as soon as they came in."

The young man was talking into his beer. There was no one on the other side of him. The tavern was crowded even though it was past midnight. The North side area police headquarters was just across the street and the shifts had changed. I needed to relax a little bit too. We had been farther up North on Foster Avenue where two police officers had been shot dead, gunned down in a tavern a block from the police station.

It was the old Summerdale District, known in infamy for some night shift cops who became burglars back in the fifty's. That's when O.W. Wilson reformed the Chicago P.D.. He didn't stay on the job very long. But that's another story.

This story was a shocker. Two uniformed cops walk into a tavern and are murdered. My camera crew and I were up there all night. But there wasn't much information. The watch commander read us a brief statement. We'd be given the names of the two victims as soon as the next of kin were notified. Why did the cops enter the tavern? Were they looking for somebody? It was all under investigation by Area Six homicide. So that's where we went after shooting exteriors of the bar. We weren't allowed inside. It was still a crime scene. There was no one around. So we shipped what we had back to the office.

It was time to go home. The overnight shift would take over. But I needed a beer to calm down. And I'm next to this kid whose mumbling about throwing darts. I sit down next to him. "What happened?" "I don't know. He seemed like an ok guy. I never saw him before. He asked if I wanted to play darts and we did. Then those cops came in the place. They had no idea. The one cop was down and the guy just kept shooting. I'm sorry. I've been talking for two hours."

"Talking to who?"

"The detective across the street."

"So you were in the tavern and saw the two policemen shot?"

This kid was pretty shook up but I had to tell him who I was and make a pitch for the story.

"I'm a reporter with Channel 5 News and I'd like to do an interview with you. Tell me what you saw."

"The detectives told me I can't talk to anybody. Im going to the grand jury first thing in the morning."

"Look, the detectives can't tell you who and who not to talk to. This is an important story. You need to record it."

"I have to think about it."

"Look, I'll meet you at the Criminal Courts Building right before you go to the grand jury. I'll have a camera crew with me. If you decide not to do it, that's OK. But you'll have the opportunity to get it off your chest."

So I went to the Criminal Courts building early the next morning. I waited a long time but the kid never showed. I went back to the office to see what the next move would be. The killer was still at large. I had to write and record what we had so far for our noon newscast. The victims were officers Bruce Garrison and William Marsek, both twenty-eight years old, both unmarried. They had joined the police department about the same time, four or five years earlier. Both men had received department commendations for good police work.

The killer was thirty year old Jacob Cohen, a thief and ex convict. He had served time in Stateville prison. Cohen had jumped bond on a recent charge of armed robbery of a suburban jewelry store where he had beaten the woman owner.

The policemen had followed him into the tavern. Perhaps they had recognized the fugitive from photographs shown at their roll call briefing.

I was shocked when I saw the story on the noon news. "A police manhunt is underway for 30-year old Jacob Cohen," said the news anchor. "Cohen is the suspected killer of two Chicago police officers last night in Raven's Tavern on Foster Avenue on the North side. But the still photo which appeared behind the anchor was not Jacob Cohen. It was Alderman Christopher Cohen, a young member of the Chicago City Council. This Cohen's father, Wilbur, had been a member of President Lyndon's Johnson's cabinet and earlier had helped get the Social Security System started. Young Christopher Cohen was a nice guy about it and accepted the station's apology for the awful mistake.

Then, in the early afternoon, a bulletin. Cohen was cornered by police and the FBI at the apartment of a girlfriend in Milwaukee. My camera crew and I left immediately for the hour and a half drive North.

There was a media frenzy when we arrived at that place, reporters and photographers everywhere. Cohen had shot and wounded an FBI agent named Richard Carr. He had fled on foot and was wounded slightly himself. He ran four blocks and entered the home of a prominent attorney, Robert Brady. It was in a beautiful neighborhood near Lake Michigan. Three of the Brady children and one of their friends were home but no adults were present. Cohen took the kids hostage. Meanwhile the FBI found a trail of Cohen's blood that led to the Brady home. Herbert Hoxie, agent in charge of the Milwaukee FBI office contacted Cohen by phone. He offered to bring a car and act as Cohen's hostage if he would let the children go. Cohen agreed but when the agent arrived the fugitive came out with fourteen year old Danny Brady, holding a gun to the boy's head. But the Brady boy showed spunk. He broke loose and dove under the waiting car. Police and FBI opened fire. Agent Hoxie was injured by shattered glass. The car lurched and the Brady boy was slightly hurt. A Milwaukee cop was wounded but survived. Jacob Cohen was hit sixteen times and lay dead. The ordeal and the carnage was over.

AN ORAL HISTORY

WHEN I COVERED *the Illinois legislature we often drove the 200 miles between Chicago and Springfield. Many times the crew and I were asked asked to stop and do a story on the way back home. Usually they were stories about agriculture. How was the corn and soybean crop doing, pigs and pork bellies? Sometimes we stumbled on a little vignette that was special.*

Fairbury, Illinois. January 1977. Conversation between a reporter and an eighty-five year old man.

So, Mr. Masterson, tell me about that cane resting by your chair. Oh, by the way, do you mind if we tape record this.

Not at all.

Go ahead and roll the tape again. OK, Mr. Masterson.

Well, I use it as a cane, but actually it's a horseman's riding stick. It was given to me by my grandfather who lived in Tennessee as a young man and then came to Illinois. It's made of hard wood, hickory, I think. See, there's a brass cup on top that comes off. At the other end is this plug that screws on. That's where they kept the mountain dew. Sometimes, in the old days, a horseman needed a bracer on a long ride. I was just a boy, a little fellow. It was 1896 and grandpa had taken me over to Pontiac where we heard William Jennings Bryant speak. He gave his famous cross of gold speech and grandpa could see I was quite taken by it. I was spellbound.

When we got home, he gave me this stick. He made me promise that, as long as I kept it, I'd be a Democrat and vote Democrat. There was one exception. If we were at war and the sitting president was of the other party, then it was ok to vote for him to show support for the country. Grandpa said he had voted for Abe Lincoln's re election during the Civil War.

He told me the riding stick was given to him by President Andrew Jackson who he had supported. When Jackson returned to Tennessee, after his first term, he gathered a group of young men, who rode with him around the territory as he campaigned for re election.

According to grandpa they ended up at Jackson's home and huge estate, The Hermitage. It was a homecoming for Jackson who had been gone a long time in Washington. There was a huge celebration, an old fashioned barbecue with music.

All of the President's supporters were given a riding stick. Jackson had many slaves at the Hermitage and many came by to welcome the President home. Grandfather told me that some slave women showed off new babies to Mr. Jackson who was very pleased as he held them. The party lasted late into the night before grandpa and the others went to bed. But he said he could hear in the distance all the negro slaves dancing and singing. He said they partied the whole night long.

*   *   *

His name was Frank Masterson, a retired postmaster of Fairbury, Illinois. I was sent to see him for an entirely different story. At the time I was s political reporter for Channel 2 (CBS) Chicago and I covered the Illinois legislature when it was in session in downstate Springfield.

They sent me an AP wire photo of Mr. Masterson sitting on

the rear bumper of his 1930 Model A Ford which he purchased in 1932 for a hundred and eighty-five dollars. The car had 200 thousand miles on it and was still going strong. The caption quoted Mr. Masterson as saying: "It's a tossup as to who will last longer, me or the car." We dutifully photographed Mr. Masterson tooling around town and then interviewed him at his home. When is was over he told me the story behind the cane or riding stick.

We broadcast the story about the Model A. But I still had the interview about Andrew Jackson and the Hermitage. I was struck by the span of History, how nearly one hundred fifty years could be connected in one story from a grandfather to his grandson.

I got one of our producers interested. We decided to enlist the help of the talented CBS artist, Marcia Danitz. She researched the Hermitage and produced a series of sketches to match Frank Masterson's story. I remember one sketch showing President Jackson passing out the riding sticks to his followers.

The piece ran about three minutes. Afterward, one of our new executive producers from out of town came by. I can't remember his name or where he was from but he was on his way to a big job in New York. "What did you think of the story," I asked him. "It was too long. I got bored."

Today I'm frequently asked whatever happened to television news. Well, people like that took it over.

A PRISONER OF WAR

JOHN ROSSI WAS the proprietor of the House of Bertini Restaurant on Wells Street, a few blocks North of the Chicago River. It was an old Italian neighborhood that had roots in the nineteenth century. Mother Cabrini worked there with the newly arrived Italian immigrants. Next door to the restaurant was the old Grand Wells Hotel, a rooming house for working men. The author Studs Terkel had grown up there.

Rossi grew up above the restaurant. His grandparents had built the building at the turn of the century and had a store that sold olive oil and other imported Italian items. John liked to tell friends his grandparents once entertained the Italian opera star Enrico Caruso.

John Rossi looked like he could have been cast as a heavy in one of the Godfather movies but he never was involved in that sort of thing. A deeply religious man, he regularly attended the nearby Assumption Church. He had been an artist at the Chicago Tribune for many years before taking over the restaurant business from relatives.

At the age of seventeen John Rossi was drafted into the Army in the middle of World War II. He was assigned to an engineering battalion and, on D Day, 1944, landed in France on Utah beach. This is how he described the experience.

"Our unit was made up mostly of young kids, draftees from

Chicago and Hamtramck, Michigan which was in the heart of the Detroit auto industry. Our job was to cut through these big hedgerows which separated the farms in that part of France.

It was hard work and occasionally we engaged the enemy in minor skirmishes. My buddy, Freddy Castrioda, got his arm shot up pretty bad. We saw a lot more combat in the skies above, German and American pilots in aerial dog fights. If our side won it was off to the races to capture the parachuting German officer. We wanted to get the pilot's sidearm, a Luger. It would bring a good price from our own officers. The guy who got the most guns was a kid named Tully from Hamtramck High School. He had been on the track team and always led the pack. If he was in the latrine the rest of us had a chance.

After one of these battles a German bailed out and we all took off across the fields. As usual Tully was far in the lead. From a distance I saw Tully encounter the German pilot. I couldn't believe my eyes. They were hugging each other and dancing around.

When the rest of us arrived at the scene, Tully introduced us to his friend who spoke fluent English. They had gone to Hamtramck High School together and both were on the track team. The German's father, an engineer, had migrated to the U.S. to work in the auto industry and the son had grown up in Hamtramck. His father, a devotee of Adolph Hitler, took the family back to Germany when Hitler gained power. His son went to college and then joined the Luftwaffe.

The two of them jabbered away about high school as we walked back to our encampment. When we got close, an officer shouted: "Why isn't that prisoner in restraints?" One of our guys replied. "It's OK, sir, he and Tully are old buddies from Hamtramck High."

THE HUNTERS

1977

THEY WERE COMING toward us through the high grass. Sometimes only their heads were visible. The combination of sunlight and waving prairie grass made a strange look. At a hundred yards I could see they were all black and young. They moved deliberately, almost in a formation. Had they seen us yet? Surely they had.

They all carried what looked to be a long weapon. I had this image in my mind of an old movie. African tribesmen on the move through the jungle, drums beating in the background. I could hear they had dogs with them. There must have been two dozen young men.

But this wasn't Africa. It was Chicago, 130th Street and the Dan Ryan Expressway. Tall grass growing in this wasteland with old grain elevators standing in the background, old monuments of another time. Amidst the grass were broken bottles, rocks and beer cans. The din of interstate traffic was deafening. It was a wonder anything could grow or live there.

They carried something else with them, around their wastes. As they came closer I could see the weapons were sawed off broom sticks with nails coming out the end, home made spears. Around their wastes were globs of furry things. Rabbits, that's what they were.

At first I was frightened. Could this be one of the street gangs that roamed this part of the city? The tough Altgeld Gardens public housing project was a stone's throw away. Gardens? That was a good one. The place was riddled with drugs, gangs and mayhem.

As it turned out these young men were from Altgeld. But they were friendly, fascinated by our camera. "Are you gonna take our picture, man?" Sure.

We were there to film the grain elevators. Pictures needed to go with a story about a big sale of American Wheat to the Russians who had a bad growing season.

They fanned out in a big circle, closing inward, beating the grass, the dogs barking. They would flush out their prey and then just chase it down. The place was loaded with rabbits. They would sell the rabbits at the Gardens for thee dollars and fifty cents each or just cook them for their families.

The Illinois Department of Conservation said it was illegal to kill rabbits with sticks, also illegal to sell them. But none of these kids has ever been caught. Someone said they've been doing it for years. I think it's much longer than that.

BREAKDOWN

I T WAS THAT stone cold look on his face. That look of defiance as he stood on the podium facing hundreds of people dressed in formal attire in the ballroom of the Palmer House Hotel.

He was holding his light meter and looking at it. A young man in his early twenties, slight of build. I had a bad feeling. But at that very moment everything seemed normal. The audience was applauding. Some were on their feet. George Schultz, the President's budget director, was approaching the podium. And they had seen this before. A photographer getting a last minute light reading.

Now the applause began to subside and Schultz was at the podium, politely waiting for the man to step aside. But he stayed where he was with his arm outstretched holding his light meter. And that stone cold look on his face.

There was just a trickle of applause now and some nervous coughing. That's when everyone else got the feeling I had a few moments before. No one, least of all Schultz, knew what to make of it. Because the young man wouldn't budge. Then there was silence. The embarrassing silence now gave way to a few snickers and giggles.

Now Schultz decided to take action. He tried to gently move the young photographer away from the podium and take his place. But he was immovable. And Schultz leaned into the microphone and tried to make light of the matter: "You know we've been having trouble with the media lately." This was during the Watergate scandal of the Nixon administration.

Someone in the office got a call from the New York desk that they wanted to cover the Schultz speech. Someone in New York had received a tip that Schultz was going to drop a bombshell that evening in Chicago. I was going to work that night, get a little overtime. I was enjoying a drink and a steak dinner at the Wagon Wheel across from the Merchandise Mart. But the nice slow evening I anticipated was not to be. The desk called and said I had to go to the Palmer House immediately. There was a problem. The crew had called and someone had stopped them from setting up.

I'll call the cameraman Jack Thomas. It's not his real name and I never saw him again after that night. He was a freelancer and I had worked with him a couple times in the past. Jack was very young and very quiet. One of the other guys had described him as brilliant but fragile.

When I arrived outside the grand ballroom, dinner guests were still enjoying cocktails. Off to the side was my camera crew, light and camera cases piled up on a dolly. Jack Thomas looked shaken, and unable to speak. The sound man told me that a Mr. Dedmon, the chairman of the event , a Mr. Dedmon, had thrown Jack out of the main ballroom as he was setting up his tripod. There would be no television coverage of Schultz's speech. According to Dedmon the lights and the camera would be too disruptive. Some harsh words were spoken and Jack was unable to respond.

Mr. Dedmon turned out to be Emmett Dedmon, vice president and Editorial Director of The Chicago Sun Times and the Chicago Daily News. He had served in the Army Air Corps in World War II. His plane was shot down over Germany and he was a prisoner of war for two years. Dedmon was a powerful man in Chicago with a powerful resume: Trustee of the University of Chicago, chairman of the Alumni fund, founding member of the Trilateral Commission, trustee of the Chicago Historical Society and on and on. This was not to be one of his better nights. And I believe he never knew the consequences of his mood swing. I'm sure he never knew he was dealing with a very sensitive and vulnerable young man.

Dedmon was pointed out to me across the room and I went over to him. I was polite because I knew who he was although I had never met the man. He seemed agitated and angry. He didn't want the secretary's speech to be marred by the carnival atmosphere that surrounded television. These were the days when print people didn't like television. I told him we had a job to do and gave him the old first amendment routine. Surely, he, of all people, could understand that.

So Mr. Dedmon relented. We could go in and cover the speech but he warned that we would be thrown out immediately at the first sign of disruption.

*   *   *

Now, as Jack Thomas stood in front of that podium, the audience was stunned. And, just as I thought the security guards would come, Jack lowered his hand. And he turned and he looked at Schultz and then at the audience and he walked away. And there was a slight smile on his face. And I knew damn well what he was saying. To hell with all of you! He walked proudly back to his camera and commenced rolling.

The rest of it was mostly a blur for me. I glanced over at Dedmon a couple of times and he glared back. I was pretty shaken myself and quickly read through the long text of the speech, frantically looking for the sound bite, the "bombshell" that someone in New York had heard about. Maybe it came from some PR person in a cocktail lounge. But it wasn't there. It was all economic gibberish. The tuxedos and their companions all nodded attentively as Schultz droned on.

Jack couldn't take any direction that night. He turned the camera on and off when he felt like it. When I talked to him it was like talking to the camera. He couldn't hear.

It was the same way as we left the office that night, as I tried to get him to talk about what had gone wrong.

Jack didn't show up for work the next day. They sent a courier over to his place but he had locked himself in. When I heard about it the worst fear came up in me again. But nothing really bad happened that day and I guess his family came and finally got him.

I used to ask about him now and then and one of the crew guys said his mother and father had sent him to a place in Arizona to rest.

The Schultz speech never made the air. Not local, Nightly News, the Today Show or even syndication. I think the film is with all the other dead stuff in a big warehouse in New Jersey. Sometimes I think of it even today when I see Schultz on television. He's an old man now, an elder statesman.

The Election

Circa 1977

I T WAS A primary election for alderman of the 18th ward
on the South side of Chicago. Bob Kellam, the endorsed
candidate of the Democratic Party organization, defeated
Andy McGann by a little less than seven hundred votes.

It was an Irish bloodletting. Neighbors went up against
neighbors, cousins against cousins, even members of the same
family took different sides. Kellam, and McGann were from the
same parish. McGann was a popular funeral director. (Is that
what that word oxymoron means?)

There was bluster and cheer at Kellam headquarters as
victory was finally assured. Not so at McGann's place. I watched
the tears streaming down Andy's cheeks as he encountered the
first painful swallows of defeat.

A stench of corruption hung over the campaign. The ward
committeeman, John Daley, a first cousin of the late Mayor,
had chosen Kellam to run. Not long before Daley had admitted,
under a grant of immunity from prosecution, that he had paid
a bribe to a County official. McGann had raised the corruption
issue in the campaign.

But Andy was outflanked by a large number of precinct
captains in the Kellam camp. They were fighting for their

livelihood, their jobs with the city, or the Park District or the County of Cook.

As always in Chicago there was a racial aspect to the story. In the 1970's the Eastern third of the 18th ward was black. The other side of Western Avenue was all white. The blacks and whites never mixed very well in that neighborhood. Border lines were respected. Out of necessity blacks and whites came together at the ward headquarters. Ironically it was the black precincts which settled the Irish dispute and put Kellam over the top.

The powerful Democratic machine prevailed once again. What the hell did a little corruption have to do with it. And the tears rolled down Andy McGann's cheeks. Some time later he would return to the fold and get elected to the state legislature.

It was the first open battle among Democrats since the passing of Mayor Richard J. Daley. A precinct worker said: "If the Mayor was alive, this never would have happened."

The Fetcher

Circa 1976

A FETCHER BILL. (DEF. *by Ogg and Ray). It is as old as the American Republic and probably has roots in older governments elsewhere. A legislator introduces a bill that might hurt or be costly to a business or industry. A representative of that business gets "fetched" to the legislator or legislators who have crafted the scheme. A deal is made and money changes hands. And poof, the harmful legislation goes away. Some states refer to it as a "juice" bill as in let's squeeze somebody and get a little juice. In the lore of most legislatures are stories of notorious fetcher bills. In Illinois there's the one about the brazen downstate senator who introduced a bill requiring that all candy sold at retail in Illinois must be wrapped in cellophane. The candy industry fetched up.*

I sat in the gallery of the Illinois House of Representatives looking down on the raucous house floor. I would go there to get away from the madness of the day.

The house gallery was above and just behind the speakers' podium. It was a little dark and visitors were few because not many people knew how to get up there. The public and the tours went to the side and rear galleries above the chamber.

I liked it there. My colleagues were below and could not see me. They sat in the press boxes on either side of the speaker's podium. I could think, and if I had a little hangover as I did this day, I might doze a bit. I had a strange notion that It was my duty to accompany legislators to saloons after adjournment. That's the way it was back then. Deadline time would come later when I would actually have to write a story for broadcast back to Chicago. But right now I enjoyed a little peace and quiet.

It was the 70's. The house had 177 members and it was very disorderly. Legislators were out of their seats wandering all over the floor. It was loud. Some people were eating fried chicken and pizza delivered to their desks by young pages. A woman member was breast feeding her baby. That stuff was in full bloom then. You could even get a stiff drink in the office of a Democratic leader, just off the house floor. Beer flowed freely in the press room. All of this pandemonium and some damn fool is trying to make a speech about the environment. Yet I found rest sitting up there. I could look down and somehow it seemed to be miles away.

I remember thinking about a milestone of sorts that had passed several years earlier in my career. I had been raised in a Democratic household. Republicans were the bad guys. My father was a precinct captain and a lawyer, a devoted follower of Franklin D. Roosevelt. He had run for congress and lost. As I practiced journalism I found I actually liked some of the Republicans I covered. And some of them had good ideas. I liked this idea of being a non partisan and objective reporter.

As I sat there looking down on this craziness we call Democracy, I happened to notice a guy reach into his lapel pocket, pull out an envelope and hand it to another man right there on the house floor. A year before I had covered a federal bribery trial in Chicago that involved payoffs to fix legislation on the weight of ready-mix cement trucks on state highways.

Could they still be taking money on the floor of the house

with the heat of such a trial so close, I wondered as an envelope disappeared into a vest pocket followed by some pats on the back and handshakes. Not a chance, I thought, with tough prosecutors following up all the scandalous newspaper articles of that time. But time would prove that they were taking dough as they always have in Illinois and other states and cities and and in the halls of congress.

That night I went and had drinks at the Statehouse Inn with Representative John Matejevich a veteran legislator from North Chicago, a man I believed to be honest. He was an independent Democrat, not afraid to go against the powerful Daley machine in Cook County to his South. He had once rebuked Daley to his face in a public party meeting, much to the chagrin of Daley loyalists in attendance. The Mayor, said John Matijevich, had been heavy handed in selecting candidates for state offices without consulting committeemen from outside of Cook County.

So that night at the Statehouse Inn in Springfield I put it right to him. "John, in all your years in the legislature, were you ever offered a bribe?" Matejevich smiled broadly. "Nah, they knew I wouldn't take it and the money boys learn that about you early on. But I'll tell you a funny story that happened when I first arrived in Springfield. It's along the lines you're talking about.

"When I came here I was naive and thought I could change a lot of things. I had been a magistrate and chief of police in North Chicago. My family had been in the tavern business for years. North Chicago was a Navy town, right by the Great Lakes base. Our family always thought the Illinois dram shop law was unfair. This is the law that allows persons injured by drunks to sue the tavern who sold the booze. We were always careful about over serving customers. And you never know about bad drinkers. They may go to other taverns or they might have booze in their car. Insurance companies made big money selling dram shop insurance.

So I introduced a bill to repeal the dram shop law. I was sincere and really meant it. It caused quite a stir. I ran into the chairman of the insurance committee in the hall one day. He was a Republican from Mayor Daley's ward. (In those days a minority party member had to be elected from each district. Usually they were with the majority.) I asked him when we could have a hearing on my bill. He replied: 'John, nobody's called me.' I was a little puzzled. I told him I really wanted to argue this cause. But every time I saw him after that the response was the same. ' Nobody's contacted me.' My bill never got a hearing in committee. It went nowhere. I think they were trying to see if I might play ball. It was my first lesson about the legislative process, democracy at work. I got the message."

MIFLIN STREET

circa 1974

*I*N THE WEE *hours of the morning of August 24, 1970, four young men drove to Sterling Hall on the University of Wisconsin campus in Madison. The stolen van they were in contained thousands of pounds of Ammonium Nitrate fertilizer and sticks of dynamite. They parked the car, lit the fuse and took off. The ensuing explosion destroyed much of the five story building and damaged many neighboring structures. 33 year old Robert Fassnacht, a physics researcher who had been working on a lower floor was killed. He left a wife and three small children. Four other people in the building were hurt.*

It was the largest act of terrorism on U.S. soil until the Oklahoma City bombing of 1995.

The four bombers, who had been students at the University were: Karlton Armstrong, his younger brother Dwight, David Fine and Leo Burt. They were protesting the Viet Nam War and specifically an Army research center housed in the building which did work for the war effort. The Armstrong brothers and David Fine were eventually arrested, convicted and given light sentences. The brothers later opened a deli restaurant in downtown Madison. Leo Burt was never found and is still on the FBI's most wanted list. Madison was a hotbed of protests against the Viet Nam War in those days. Some of them were violent. I was sent to cover one of those events not long after the Sterling Hall explosion

The street was filled with happy young college students, many of whom were intoxicated that Sunday afternoon in Wisconsin. I was strolling along, taking it all in. My camera crew would arrive a little later. At this time everyone was in the happy phase.

A young woman came toward me. She was eating something from a bowl in her hands. "Want some oatmeal," she asked with a smile and eyes a little hazy. "No thanks."

It was an old neighborhood with old homes and two flats, mostly populated by students but some families also lived there. There were parties and demonstrations all the time. When my crew came we decided to have dinner since the activities on Miflin Street were just getting started.

When we returned the whole scene was starting to go nuts. Hundreds of students packed the street, many of them stoned out of there minds. The smell of the weed permeated the area They had started huge bonfires in the middle of the street.

Then the Dane County sheriff's police showed up. But it wasn't the type of confrontation I was used to seeing. There must have been a half dozen clunker cars all covered with wire mesh. They drove down the street plowing into the fires. The students threw bottles and bricks at the cops to no avail. This frustrated them even further. When they had the chance the police threw out some tear gas bombs. I remember thinking the cops are as crazy as the demonstrators

We shipped a bunch of film back to Chicago for the ten o'clock news.

As the evening wore on the crowd diminished. The tear gas was just too much. The fires died down. The crew and I decided to call it a day. I asked for a 7 AM call so we could come back and film the aftermath.

The next morning you could still smell the tear gas and the marijuana. There was debris all over the street and it was quiet as we took pictures. Then something surprising happened. People started coming out of the houses and walking down the street. They were well dressed, going to work or school. I stopped one man to ask what it was like to live there. As the camera rolled, he told me it was bad, very bad. Trouble, police noise, sometimes violence on a regular basis. Then he had to excuse himself. He had to catch a bus for work. I wondered if he had a family and what that was like living on Miflin Street.

When I think back on it today that morning after scene on Miflin Street, on a much smaller scale, was like London when the Nazis were bombing constantly. And each morning the Brits would come out of their holes, catch trains and go to work.

They still have parties in the Spring and I always ask about that when I meet a student from the University. There's music and drinking. Sometimes it gets rowdy and police are called. But it's not as bad as that Sunday I was there so many years ago and that terrible war was still going.

PROVIDENCE ST. MEL

Circa 1977

I KIND OF GOT *labeled us the Catholic reporter in the 1970's both at NBC and the three years I was over at CBS. Very much a sinner, I still had quintessential Catholic credentials: Twelve years of Catholic education , St. Rose of Lima grade school and Canisius (Jesuit) H.S. in Buffalo, N.Y., Villanova (Augustinian) University. I had a sister who was a nun. At a time when the country was worried about the environment and the population explosion I was the father of six kids . When my wife was pregnant with the sixth she told of getting some dirty looks as she walked down the street in our nice suburb with the other five in tow. That was on Earth Day. There were many Catholic Church stories in Chicago at the time, school and church closings, young priests demonstrating at Cardinal Cody's office. This was long before the priest abuse scandals came to light. So when newsroom producers and assignment types wanted to cover these events the usual response was: Send Nolan. He used to be an altar boy.*

"The school is a loser. There's no money. The building is old and in need of repairs. Most of the kids going there aren't even Catholic. We just can't afford it." The man I was interviewing was the Vicar General of the Roman Catholic Archdiocese of

Chicago. I was sent to him to get some official response to a story I had done earlier about the efforts of a small group of people, parents, alumni, a dedicated staff and a heroic principal, who wanted to save the school.

Providence High School was founded in 1929 by the Sisters of Providence and combined with St. Mel's, a Christian Brothers High School for boys in 1969. If you look at the yearbooks of High Schools on the West side of Chicago in the 1950's you can see in the class photos the neighborhood quickly turning from white to black.

The Gothic Providence St. Mel school building was still there but the neighborhood was impoverished. Drug dealers, gangs, pimps and prostitutes were all around.

I was sent out to the school to see what was happening and record a story. The Principal was Paul Adams, a very strong and determined looking guy. We strolled through the corridors and visited classrooms. My crew and I were greeted by students who looked like they enjoyed being there. The girls were dressed in uniforms, the boys in shirts and ties. What struck me most was how quiet it was. As a newsman I had visited schools for one reason or another, and I had taught for one year in a public junior high school. There was a lot of noise and traffic in the schools I had been in. This place was different. You could feel the discipline. There were strict rules, no gang affiliation, no loitering in the corridors, no drugs.

Young teachers, some of them religious, some lay, had come from other parts of the country to work in this school. They were enthusiastic. So was the Principal, Mr. Adams. He had come to the school to volunteer as a counselor. He was a successful young black businessman, a role model. Adams had a life changing experience. He believed these kids deserved a chance and he decided to work at the school full time. Adams had owned a popular chain of chicken restaurants on the

Souths side. His wife couldn't understand why he was giving it all up. She divorced him. Paul Adams became the Principal of Providence St. Mel.

We had filmed the neighborhood surrounding the old school. Within a couple blocks there was a pretty nasty looking tavern. Prostitutes and tough looking idlers milled about in broad daylight. I had asked Adams how he kept the kids away from that or how he kept those people away from the kids. "Every so often I go over there and let them know they are to stay away from the school and the students. They have heard me."

Mr. Adams had planted grass and shrubs and flowers around the school and they survived. You didn't see such things around the schools in that part of Chicago. Graduates of Providence St. Mel's were getting accepted at top universities.

Parents became involved in the school. Fundraisers were organized. Alumni began helping. Someone put an ad in the Wall Street Journal telling the Providence-St. Mel story and its need to survive. An alumnus named Flavin, who owned race horses, said he would donate the winnings of one of his horses at Sportsmans Park. We later went out to the track to cover the race. The horse finished in the money.

Our story of this unique high school was picked up by the CBS Network. They sent me to get reaction from Cardinal Cody when he was presiding at an outdoor ceremony at Holy Name Cathedral. Can you imagine, my camera crew and I chasing the Cardinal Archbishop in his mitre and vestments? He escaped without saying a word. I have to admit I was somewhat relieved. I thought I might get excommunicated.

The Archdiocese of Chicago did end its relationship with the school. But Providence St. Mel survived. Good things started to happen. Mike Leonard of NBC News told the story to a national audience. President Ronald Reagan, who wanted to end the welfare state, visited the school twice. A grade school was established.

Over the years Providence St. Mel has received a half ton of awards and accolades including a state basketball championship.

CHICAGO HOUSING AUTHORITY

Circa 1969

*I*N 1969 THE *Chicago Cubs were contenders for their division title in the National League. When I came back to the newsroom every day there was a lot of buzz around the assignment desk. The Cubbies did it again today. Fergie had his stuff. Ernie put another one out and did you see Santo? But true to form in those days the Cubs began to fade in September. The New York Mets took over. I was involved in a Federal Court case called Gautreaux versus the Chicago Housing Authority. It had to do with the perennial and persistent problem of racial integration in the city which Dr. King had called the most segregated in the nation.*

The city had an idea to improve the housing of poor African Americans that may have been conceived with good intentions, although it perpetuated the notion that white Chicagoans didn't want poor blacks living in their neighborhoods. Street and railroad track boundaries of the black neighborhoods were sharply drawn, first on the South side and later on the West side.

For the poorest of the poor, the city decided to provide shelter in high rise public housing projects. They were managed by a government created entity known as the Chicago Housing Authority. From the late 1940's through the 50's and into the 60's the city built 168 high rise buildings which once housed over 19 thousand residents. They ranged from fifteen to nineteen stories, high and were often named after prominent citizens or politicians.

The Robert Taylor homes ran for many blocks along the South side between State Street and the Dan Ryan Expressway. Henry Horner Homes were near the Eisenhower Expressway on the West side. Then there was the infamous Cabrini Green Project on the near North Side within walking or running distance of the fashionable Gold Coast neighborhood. It was the backdrop for a popular television sitcom of the 1970's, Good Times. There were the Abla Homes on Roosevelt Rd., Lathrop Homes, a low rise development on the North side had housed the poor whites of public housing. All the rest were predominantly black.

On occasion I was assigned to go into these projects with a camera crew. The crews required a bodyguard because you never knew what might happen in there. The guard was usually an off duty Chicago cop, armed with his service revolver. I didn't blame the crews. They were defenseless for the most part. The cameraman had a heavy camera mounted to his chest on a steel brace. The sound guy, with his recording gear, was attached to the camera with what they called an umbilical cord.

What I remember most was the stench when you entered one of these places, a powerful combination of urine and a mix of food cooking odors. The urine dominated. Then there were the sounds, babies whaling, mothers screaming at children. The elevators were all graffiti and sometimes didn't work. Gang members roamed about at will, usually on the over night shift.

Most of the residents were on welfare, most of them single

mothers. They were entitled to a monthly payment for each dependent child, the more children, the more money. This fostered a system whereby wandering men visited the projects and helped create more children. Few of the men ever stayed.

For most people in the projects life was a dead end street. Young males joined the gangs at an early age, got into drugs, armed robbery, rape and even murder. They ended up in prison for long stretches. I remember doing a story about the Black Panthers providing free bus service for project mothers to go see their sons in maximum security prisons downstate.

Police patrolled the area, but like repairmen and everyone else, didn't like to go up in the buildings. Any vacant apartments were controlled by the gangs and were used as hangouts for drug trafficking. Sometimes they were the scene of unspeakable crimes.

For years after the federal court ruled the high rise buildings were unlawful, they were still in use. In 2006 a beautiful young blonde woman arrived at Midway Airport from California. She was suffering from bi-polar disorder and her behavior was erratic. Somehow she got on public transportation and ended up in a neighborhood near the Robert Taylor Homes. She was causing a disturbance on the street. Police arrested her and took her to a nearby station. The twenty-one year old was held for forty-eight hours. Despite calls from her parents, who told of her condition, police released her all alone into the neighborhood. She ended up in a project apartment where she was beaten and raped. She either jumped or was pushed from from a seventh floor balcony. Despite multiple injuries the young woman survived. But she was totally disabled and mute. The family filed suit and eventually won a twenty-two million dollar award from the city.

Despite the overwhelming odds, many people survived the projects. That blessed institution of motherhood often took over. Moms who wanted something better for their kids got them into programs like Head Start. I did a story on a veteran teacher named Anne Noone at the Oakenwald School in the shadow of the projects. She started tutoring interested students after school. The day we were with her she was visited by two young men, former students who were attending Notre Dame and Princeton.

Jesse White founded a gymnastics team called the Jesse White Tumblers, a club that offered project kids of all ages the opportunity to do something positive. Members had to maintain a C average in school and stay away from, drugs, alcohol and gangs. Jesse White believed in giving back to the community. An all round athlete himself, White became one of the most successful and classier politicians in Chicago. He was elected State Representative, Recorder of Deeds and Secretary of State. The Jesse White tumblers still perform all over the world.

Many years after covering the Chicago Housing Authority Mike Houlihan and I produced a show that included two comedians from the Second City troop, Michael McCarthy and Greg Holliman. Both were gifted actors and very funny. Holliman was a tall lanky African American. I remember asking him where he had grown up and he told me Cabrini-Green. How did you manage that? I asked. He told me in the years they lived there his mother never let him out of the apartment alone. She was always with him.

In 1969 a Federal Judge named Richard B. Austin issued a ruling in the Gautreux versus Chicago Housing Authority case. Judge Austin said essentially that the warehousing of black tenants in high rise buildings in segregated neighborhoods violated their civil rights protected by the U.S. Constitution. Judge Austin said any future units constructed by the CHA must be on scattered sites in integrated neighborhoods. There was resistance from the city. Appeals were made and the case dragged on.

I would cover many hearings on the matter The attorney for the plaintiffs was Alexander Polikoff who lived in a fashionable North Shore suburb. I used to see him on the train and then in court. He worked tirelessly in behalf of his inner city neighbors. Polikoff would later write a book about the case.

I was sent to interview project moms about the issue. How do you feel about going to smaller units in white neighborhoods? I remember one woman at the Abla Homes who answered this way: Why would I want to go out and live with whitey if whitey don't want me."

The litigation would go on for over thirty years, the longest case in the history of the U.S. Court for the Northern District of Illinois. Judge Austin died in 1977. Other Judges took over the case , retired and passed it on. But eventually those project buildings went down and the city complied with the court order. I had retired from broadcasting, grown old and had a mess of grand children.

There was one comical footnote to the story that typified the zany nature of Chicago politics. Judge Richard B. Austin was a Democrat. He had an impressive legal resume and was appointed to the federal bench by President John F. Kennedy. This could not have happened without the blessing of Mayor Daley. Daley accused the Judge of embarrassing him and the city with his public housing decision. The Judge countered that he was only interested in the law.

Judge Austin was a member and officer of the Olympia Fields Country Club in the far Southern reaches of Cook County. Olympia Fields is one of the top golf courses in the nation and has hosted many tournaments including the U.S. Open. Like many clubs there were card games in the evening where money changed hands. One night in 1971 the Cook County Sheriff's police raided the place and arrested some of the members.

Judge Austin publicly claimed foul and said the raid was in retaliation for his ruling against the Housing Authority. He challenged the Sheriff to take a lie test and say it wasn't so. But that never happened.

THE FISHERMAN

Circa 1974

H IS NAME WAS Gaetano Terranova and his people came
from Sicily. They had been fishermen for generations,
as long as anyone could remember. When they came to
this country they came first to California where they fished the
Pacific Ocean. Somehow Gaetano ended up at the great inland
sea, Lake Michigan. He fished for Yellow Perch and Chub from
a steel hulled boat that looked like a box in the water.

Terranova was very respectful of the Lake. "On the ocean,"
he told me, "the storms come and go abruptly. They are more
predictable. Here on the Lake it can be very rough. You never
know."

I was to find this out personally when I was assigned to
Terranova's boat for a story about fishing licenses. The state
of Illinois wanted to restrict the number of commercial
fishing licenses it issued because of declining Perch and Chub
populations in the Lake.

It was May and the weather was breaking as usual in Chicago,
still cold, but lots of sunshine. One of my editors kept asking
about the fishing license story, Where was it. I had to tell him
the fisherman, Terranova, kept insisting the weather was not
good enough for us to make the trip. The editor kept pointing

to the sunshine. Finally Terranova gave me a day although he advised the lake might still be rough.

The day came clear and we drove to Jo's Fishery on the Chicago River where the boat was docked. A cameraman, sound technician, light man and I boarded the crude vessel in what looked to be a fun assignment. It was not to be.

We proceeded down the river, through the locks East of Michigan Avenue and out into the Lake. It was still a sunny day but the lake was angry. Large waves knocked us dizzy right away. In those days many of the union film technicians were older men, some were World War II veterans. Many were near retirement. On this boat my sound man was past seventy. The electrician (lights) was in his sixties. My cameraman was in his thirties like me. None of us had sea legs.

We began filming. Within minutes the electrician turned white and began throwing up all over. Crew members tried to get him to do it in an opening on the side of the boat. I looked at my cameraman. He too was turning white. The boat pitched back and forth. Then the sound man started heaving. My cameraman tried to be strong but finally he became nauseous. Then I thought I might go. I was very close.

So here was this NBC crew, totally disabled. And the waves never ceased The fishing crew was sympathetic but they had to get to their nets. When we got there the crew started pulling in the nets. It was quite a scene, all these fish spilling into the hold of the boat. George Peebles was one of our great cameramen. He pulled himself together and managed to get some good footage. The other two guys were able to settle down. To my surprise, I began to feel a little better.

What a relief when Terranova told us we were headed for home. I think we were about 20 miles out in the lake. Outside the sunny skies had turned to a thick fog. They had to use radar to find an opening in the breakwater.

Going up the river I noticed crew members gutting and cleaning a mess of Perch. "That'll be your lunch," Terranova told me. I wasn't sure I could eat anything. By the time we reached Jo's fishery we were all pretty hungry. And that fresh fried lake Perch may have been one of the best things I ever tasted. I wish I could remember the name of the boat.

Many years later I read a story in the Tribune that Gaetano Terranova was one of three crew members who survived the sinking of a boat called the Searcher in the icy waters of Lake Michigan. He must have lost his own boat and license years before. When he reached the hospital Gaetano's body temperature was 84 degrees. Three other crew members were lost. They go down to the sea in ships.

INHERITANCE

Circa 1963

M Y FATHER, RALPH W. Nolan died in 1948 at the age of 51. I was just short of nine years old. My brother was eleven. My sister was eighteen and had recently entered the convent of the Grey Nuns of the Sacred Heart in Philadelphia.

Dad was a Workers Comp lawyer. He helped working people get just compensation for injuries sustained on the job. My father hadn't been able to practice law the past couple of years before he died due to his continuing heart disease. Before he got real sick he wanted to take his family on the train to Philadelphia to visit my sister the new nun. So he borrowed money from an old client to do it. The man, George Gruehler, had lost a leg in an industrial accident and Dad won him a big settlement. Later Dad ended up in the veterans hospital in Batavia, New York where he died on June 18th. (My father was drafted into the Navy in 1917. World War I soon ended and he was discharged.)

After his death my Mother said she found two copper pennies in one of his suit coat pockets. That was it. But we survived. Mom got a job at Merchants Mutual Insurance where she had met Dad, a young lawyer, in the 1920's. My brother Mike and I got odd jobs, shoveling snow, delivering papers.

It must have been a struggle but my Mom managed to send brother Mike and me to Canisius, a Jesuit High School. The tuition was two hundred dollars a year. Mom was always broke and a master at finding consolidated debt loans. I can still see her fiddling with the payment books.

Mom's brother, Uncle Eddie Way, had a thriving pinball machine business in Detroit. He bought us our first television set and later bought Mom a car. My Dad's sister, Aunt Mamie, was also pretty well off. Once, at the pleading of my sister, she paid off my mothers tangle of small debt.

Aunt Mamie would send me to Villanova University in Philadelphia. Brother Mike went into the Air Force for four years, got the GI bill and parlayed it into an education at Michigan State University. My mother always advised us not to become lawyers. "Your Dad was a good lawyer, but too soft. He never charged enough for his work."

I've lived a lot longer than my father and, thankfully, was able to provide a good education for my children who are all doing well as adults. Once, when I was a young newsman, I had a chance to gather some big time wealth.

When I started work at WHLD Radio in Niagara Falls, New York, a new phenomenon had come upon the American scene, the fifteen cent hamburger. I was familiar with a couple of them, Henry's and Carroll's. A guy named Ray Kroc, who sold milkshake machines, started a chain called McDonalds. It was fast food. A young newsman like me could get a burger, fries and a coke, eat and be on my way in under ten minutes. It wasn't like today where you have to stand around for awhile or wait in a drive through line. You handed them the money and they gave you the bag. This was before everything got computerized.

Our station had one main salesman. His name was Walter Allen. He had one arm, having lost the other in an auto accident when he was in college. Walt was a great guy and I really looked up to him. Despite his disability he was a terrific athlete. He was city paddle ball champion. The one arm was like a sledge hammer. And he always outdrove me the few times we played golf. This would cause stares from other golfers wondering how this one armed guy was out driving a man about twenty years his junior.

I drove a station wagon boldly decorated with our station's call letters. Walt was always trying to hustle me to bring the wagon to some PR event being put on by one of his commercial clients. I dutifully declined, explaining we had to protect the integrity of the news department. Yes, I was very young and thought everything was on the square.

One day, after one of my newscasts, Walter Allen came into my office and closed the door.. "Pete, you've got a wife and little daughter, have you ever thought of investing in your family's future?" I had to admit I hadn't thought about it very much. I had been concentrating on the job, gathering news. I had an insurance policy but not much spare cash. I was only making $105 per week. I wondered why he was asking.

"I've got a new client. His name is Stan Terryberry and he's got a new hamburger place out on Pine Avenue. Stan says he thinks this business is going to take off. We could get a franchise for twenty-five thousand dollars and he would manage it for us. I'm trying to find five guys who can come up with five grand apiece. Why don't you think about it. It might be a nice financial ticket for your future."

At that time five thousand dollars could have been five hundred thousand. I thought about it for a very short time. Maybe I could have borrowed it from my Aunt Mamie or somebody else. But I nixed that idea. Aunt Mamie had already paid for my college. Within a few days I went back to Walt and told him I wasn't interested. I was a journalist and had important things to do. I wasn't interested in hamburgers.

I don't know if Walt ever got a franchise and I never asked. I was too busy. I was a newsman.

Fast forward about twenty years. I'm in a pretty high profile position as a commentator for WMAQ-TV (NBC). TV reporters, in the early days, didn't get much face time on the tube. Maybe a brief standupper at the end of the story. Then in the 70's they started putting reporters on the news set so he or she could chat with the anchors. I remember being looked at on elevators. Where have I seen this guy before? Being on the ten o'clock news doing commentary every night was an even higher profile. I started getting invited to big dinners. The station encouraged attendance because of the publicity value.

One night I found myself sitting next to Mike Quinlan, the head guy at McDonalds Corporation. He was a very friendly dinner companion so I told him about my chance to become a McDonalds owner way back when in Niagara Falls. He got a big kick out of it. "Yes, yes," he said, that's exactly what the franchises sold for in 1963, twenty-five thousand dollars." That night they were worth more than a million.

I often think of my father today and how he must have felt as his life slipped away and he knew he could do nothing to provide for the future of his family. Looking back he gave us a lot more than he or the rest of us realized at the time. When I go there will be a little more than two cents. But nobody will get rich to the tune of a McDonalds franchise.

A TIP FROM THE FBI

Circa 1970

*I*T'S JUNE OF 1968 *and I'm in the Chicago Press Club in the penthouse of the St. Clare Hotel on Chicago's Gold Coast. I'm not yet thirty years old. I've got five years experience in broadcast news behind me. I've just been hired as a wrier at WMAQ-TV news. Maybe I'm a little cocky. I'm attending an alumni cocktail party for Villanova University outside Philadelphia and I'm making acquaintances with fellow graduates who are living and working in the Chicago area. I run into a guy who I knew casually at school, a football player named John Osborne. "So what are you doing out here John?"*

"I was transferred out here, I'm with the FBI." "Wow!" I say, and then say something pretty stupid. "You know, maybe we could work together, I'm a newsman at NBC." Osborne takes me aside to make sure no one is listening. "Pete, J. Edgar Hoover runs the FBI with an iron fist. If I'm ever seen talking to a reporter I could be pounding a beat out in Wyoming." I got the message and later found out you rarely got anything out of the FBI. Their standard response to a news inquiry was: "This is an ongoing criminal investigation and we have no comment." But later, long after J. Edgar Hoover's death, John Osborne would give me a valuable tip on a big story.

Fred Hubbard was elected Alderman of the second ward on Chicago's near South side in 1969. It was a special election and Hubbard defeated the candidate of the powerful Democratic Party organization. It was a time when the city's African American community was questioning its long allegiance to the Democratic Party. Hubbard was definitely billed as a reformer when he took his seat on the City Council. He was forty years old, a handsome, articulate man. Hubbard was seated next to Alderman Fred Roti, alderman of the first ward, believed by many to be the home of Chicago's organized crime community.

Fred Roti was a very capable and influential politician. He had been on the Council for many years and before that had served in the state legislature. Roti became Fred Hubbard's mentor and convinced him it would be in his best interest to align with the Democratic Party. So Hubbard began voting for Mayor Daley's programs. Soon there was a nice payoff. Hubbard was given a 25 thousand dollar a year job to head up a federal program aimed at getting minorities into the construction trades. It seemed like a win win for everybody except for one thing. Fred Hubbard had a gambling problem.

It was page one news. Fred Hubbard was missing and so was about 100,000 dollars from the Chicago Plan, the federal jobs program that he had directed. It went on for weeks. We learned everything possible about the man. Once in awhile there would be a sighting in Las Vegas but the FBI couldn't nab him. Hubbard had vanished in May of 1971. By the end of August 1972 the Hubbard story was all but forgotten. On a Sunday night, the last day of my vacation, the phone rang at my house. " Nolan, you're do back from vacation tomorrow, right? Right. "Well, don't come to the office. Go directly to O'Hare airport. You'll meet a courier who'll have a plane ticket and some money. I'll give you details in the morning. You're going to L.A. The FBI just arrested Fred Hubbard.

I was excited. I had never been to the West Coast. I worked out of the NBC News office in Burbank. The FBI held a rare news conference. I remember all the Chicago media being there. Jay McMullen, an old time reporter for the Chicago Daily News with a flair for color wanted to know what cards Hubbard was holding when they grabbed him. The FBI didn't know. Hubbard had been arrested at a poker parlor in Gardena, an L.A. suburb that had legal card game gambling. Hubbard was sitting at one of the tables when they pinched him. We dutifully went and filmed the poker place. The next day Hubbard appeared before a Federal Judge downtown. Bond was set at fifty thousand dollars. An NBC artist made sketches of the brief proceedings and we filmed those too.

The cans of film were put in an onion bag and a courier came and took the package to the airport. We were on deadline to make one of the newscasts. We had a three hour time advantage on the coast but that was wiped out by the flight back. I remember the schedule was tight. We found out later one of my competitors, Les Brownlee, of ABC, Channel 7 ran into some bad luck. His courier was a no show. So Les had to rush his film out to the airport at the last minute. He was too late to make the deadline at Railway Express which shipped on the airlines in those days. So he ran out to the gate for the Chicago plane. He convinced a passenger to carry the onion bag with the silver cans on board. He told the person a courier would be at the gate to pick the bag up in Chicago. Unfortunately a flight attendant was suspicious when she saw the orange bag. Plane hijackings were a threat at the time. Under questioning the passenger admitted the package came from a stranger who claimed to be a TV reporter. The flight attendant took the bag to the Captain who opened a window and threw it onto the tarmac. So Channel 7 had no film that night.

My office wanted a second day story and I wanted to stay

another day. When leaving the NBC News office I could see people lining up for the Johnny Carson show. I was getting into the Hollywood scene. But there wasn't any new material to work with. We had done the poker parlor and the court appearance. Hubbard was still in jail. So I called John Osborne at the FBI office in Chicago. "John, I've never asked you for anything. Hoover is dead. I'm on the Hubbard story. If I could just get an address where he was living in L.A. it would be a big deal." Osborne took my number and, within a short time, called back with an address where Fred Hubbard had been living at the time of his arrest. It was a cottage on the back of a lot in the Watts section. When I arrived with my crew I knocked on the door. A gruff voice came from inside. "Get out of here. You can't come in." I took a chance and opened the door. There was John O'Brien a veteran crime reporter for the Chicago Tribune with a big grin on his face. "There's nothing here Pete. It's empty, just an old copy of the Tribune and a couple of marijuana butts." So we filmed the place with a closeup of the newspaper and the weeds. I interviewed a neighbor lady who had good things to say about Fred. He had taken time to play with her children. I remember her saying that he walked real tall.

So I had my second day story and shipped it back to Chicago. My cameraman gave me a nice tour of Hollywood and I had a good dinner before leaving town the next day. Fred Hubbard was later sentenced to two years in prison, served his time and got a job driving a cab.

JUSTICE

Circa 1975

*I*N CHICAGO *I covered some very interesting trials and witnessed some outstanding and not so good lawyering. This one in 1977 was a real shocker.*

I remember how stunned the courtroom was when the verdict was read. Everyone seemed surprised, especially the defendant, Chicago policeman James Loughnane. He was found not guilty of the attempted murder of his sixteen year old son, Michael. A report on Channel 2 the night before summed up the evidence. " For nearly five hours forty year old James Loughnane was on the witness stand. And in a hoarse and faltering voice he told about the afternoon of June 29th, 1975 when he and his son Michael had spent several hours in their boat on Lake Michigan. Under questioning by his attorney, Edward Genson, Loughnane told the jury how he was driving the boat toward Jackson Harbor. He heard a thump, turned and his son was gone. And, with his first wife and accusing son looking on, the defendant told how he had difficulty getting through to the Coast Guard. Were you able to use your emergency police training? Genson asked him. Breaking into tears Loughnane answered:I didn't use my police training, I panicked. Did you hit your son with a pipe, did you try to murder him? No sir I did not. Under cross examination by prosecutor John Mannion, Loughnane admitted he was the principal beneficiary on a 240 thousand dollar life insurance policy taken out on his son. He said he couldn't remember telling any story other than his son had fallen out of the boat. Mannion: Do you remember telling a police officer you went into the water after your son and saying here feel me I'm wet? Loughnane: I don't recall telling him that sir. The prosecution presented some final rebuttal witnesses late this afternoon. The bizarre case is expected to go to the jury after final arguments tomorrow."

There had been testimony that the boy had a lump on his head after he was rescued from the lake. Young Michael had testified that his father hit him on the head with a lead pipe then threw him overboard to drown. The boy treaded water for an hour before he was picked up by a sail boat.

James Loughnane had a troubled family life. He had divorced Michael's mother and remarried. Michael and a younger sister had come to live with his father and the new wife in a sixty thousand dollar home in Arlington Heights. The police department would fire Loughnane when it was disclosed he was living outside the city, a violation of department regulations.

Michael was devastated by the verdict and was led out of the courtroom by prosecutors and Judge Robert Slodowski. His father went before cameras to say how elated he was. The jury, which had deliberated two and a half hours had trouble with reasonable doubt. One woman, who said she voted guilty on the first ballot, said at the end it was the son's word against the father's. Nobody got killed. She had doubt.

STATEVILLE PRISON RIOT

1973

WE WERE OUTSIDE *on the front lawn of the Stateville maximum security prison near Joliet Illinois. There was a riot going on inside in B House. Renegade prisoners had taken guards as hostages. We were a mob of reporters, still photographers and camera crews. We couldn't go inside and there was no information available so everybody was jumpy. A car pulled up and a priest or minister with a collar got out. He was a prison chaplain. One of the geniuses in our midst stuck a microphone in his face and said dramatically: "Reverend, What's going on in there?" "I don't know," he replied. "I'm going in to see." (We had a few of those types in those days. Today they're all over the media.)*

We shipped reports into the early newscasts and it became a stakeout. Later that night the media was invited into the prison. The prisoners had agreed to release their ten hostages if they could voice their complaints to prison officials in the presence of the media.

Two hundred extra guards and state troopers, equipped with tear gas and riot gear, were prepared to storm cell house B. before the truce was negotiated. So the media rambled into the prison for a meeting between a committee of inmates and prison officials including the Director of the Illinois Department of Corrections, Alyn Sielaff. It was late. We had been outside for hours. Camera people and reporters were tired by the time the cameras and microphones were set up. Nobody could feed the ten o"clock newscasts because it was past deadline. In those days we were using sixteen millimeter color film which had to be processed in downtown Chicago at least an hour away.

So everyone settled in and the meeting went on. And it went on and on for three hours. Everybody seemed to have gotten their stuff in the first hour or so. The usual nasty complaints of inmates about conditions in their cells and brutality by prison guards. We had shots of the prison bosses listening dutifully. Print reporters went out to find phones. It looked like the story was wrapping up but the dialogue went on. Cameras were shut down and their operators sat down. A few reporters began to doze off. I admit I was in kind of a daze. Then something happened. A prisoner from Peoria named George Carney, 37 years old, began to speak. He was a white man who looked tougher than nails. He he was serving time for manslaughter, his second time in the pen. And he summed up the inmates' troubles with great emotion before a news media that was half asleep. "Today I'm an animal and I didn't used to be. Today I could kill any other human being and not feel anything... I do know what I've heard from you tonight, Mr. Sielaff, and it's the same kind of talk and evasions I've heard for the past fourteen years..I haven't been impressed by you and I do believe these men (guards) will beat me like they always have when we leave this room. If these men (inmates) had not been a whole lot saner than me, had a few more people like me been here, you wouldn't have got your officers out because we would have killed them."

Another inmate, Sam Early, African American, 38 years

old, serving nine years for armed robbery, said this: "You see, you have officers that could have lost their lives. But you were ashamed to show the public Cell House B where the taxpayers are supporting the cages that we live in. You'd rather sacrifice your officers' lives, your inmate lives than let the news media see the debased conditions we live in...in one particular cell four or five inmates may hold one inmate down while another one performs homosexual sports on him...while the captains watch through the door because this is their sport."

From Corrections Director Sielaff: " I think many of the inmates have seen some progress and feel some hope you would help us bring about improvements rather than do things that endanger the lives of our people and other inmates."

I was stunned and surprised because the media in the room were still groggy. Most of the cameras were shut down. I looked over at my own cameraman, Jim Stricklin. I was thrilled to see him up at the eye piece and rolling. He had captured every word.

The story was huge, front page. Not all the TV people had those startling sound bites which we had. The print and radio people were OK cause they traded stuff. Thanks to my alert cameraman, Stricklin, we did what I liked to call the network hat trick the next day. The Stateville riot story was on the Today show, NBC News Program Service which went to affiliates around the country, NBC Nightly News and the Eleventh Hour feed which went to all NBC affiliates.

It was not long before George Carney was being called the Animal of Stateville.

Tom Fitzpatrick, a columnist for the Chicago Sun Times seemed to sympathize with the inmates, and their plea that prison life made them less than human. Mike Royko of the Chicago Daily News looked at some of their records. He reported that Gorge Carney and Sam Early had been in and out of prison for years, convicted of crimes that grew more and more violent. Carney, he said, had held up a gas station and beat the attendant over the head with a black jack. Later, in a street fight he shot a man to death. Sam Early went to the home of an acquaintance, pointed a gun at him and demanded money. When the man said he didn't have any, Early shot him in the arm. He managed to scrounge up eight dollars and Early shot him twice in the head . Somehow the victim survived. Later police arrested Early and took him to the hospital where the victim identified him. "You always were a squealer," Early was quoted as saying, "I should have killed you."

The leaders of the riot were moved to maximum security at the old Joliet Prison. There was no other punishment. They later complained that not much had changed in prison life and there would be more bloodshed in the future.

In 1974 George Carney was back at Stateville Prison for psychiatric evaluation. One day he piled old newspapers, bed sheets and other debris at the front of his cell and set it afire. He suffered third degree burns over forty percent of his body and died later in the hospital. A prison official said: "He obviously was a very angry and confused man who had been in trouble all his life."

CITY SAVINGS and LOAN

Circa 1972

I COVERED MANY STORIES *about the City Savings and Loan scandal in the early 1970's. There were court hearings and community meetings and sad interviews with the victims. It was a real heart breaker. Sixteen thousand depositors lost 28 million dollars in savings when the company failed. Mostly they were working people, immigrants from Eastern Europe who had put their life savings in the place. They were scrub women who cleaned buildings and construction workers, laborers. They liked City Savings because they got premiums for their deposits, toasters, mix masters, even TV sets if the account was big enough. Everything was gone when the City Savings closed in 1964. So was the head man, C. Orin Mensik, like many of his depositors, an immigrant from Eastern Europe. Only Mensik was a smooth talking swindler who knew his way around political circles and around the law. I still have a thick file on the case including a report by a state commission which investigated what happened. It found that state regulators had been derelict in their supervision of City Savings and Loan. Mensik had conned them.*

What I remember most was the old women in babushkas crying and screaming in the Federal courtroom. Were they really that old or was it the look of long, hard labor carved on their faces. The hearing was brief. Federal Judge William Campbell read a short history of the case. But there wasn't much else to do because one of the the court appointed attorneys for the receivers was ill. There must have been a hundred people crowded into the courtroom. One woman asked the Judge why the sick attorney had received 160 thousand dollars to date while the depositors had received nothing. Judge Campbell told her the lawyer had earned the fees he received. One woman said: " I scrubbed floors for fifteen years so the crooks could get my money." Then all the women cried: Crooks! Crooks! Some of them banged umbrellas on the benches. I think the Judge might have been frightened as he gaveled the hearing to a close and hustled out of the courtroom.

Orin Mensik had been sentenced to prison on an unrelated insurance fraud case. But he had walked away from a federal prison farm in Pennsylvania and hadn't been seen since. Many believed he fled to Switzerland to be close to the 20 million dollars he diverted from City Savings into an account there. The State of Illinois had failed the depositors miserably. It allowed the institution to remain open even after Mensik's questionable practices were well known. Mensik was even able to get legislation passed to permit new deposits in 1959 when City Savings was hopelessly unsound. The accounts were never insured although Mensik proclaimed they were.

The case dragged on for years. Once in awhile there would be a newspaper item that Mensik had been seen in the Bahamas or some other glamorous place. Victims got old and some died. One depositor was June Bellino, a housewife whose daughter Cathy had been blind since birth. Her husband was semi retired after being a painter for twenty years. They all had a joint account of fifteen thousand dollars that went South. Anthony Schmendera lost money when a bank failed in Cleveland in

1929. Thirty years later he made the mistake of putting money in City Savings.

The lawyers made out OK as they usually do. About a million dollars in recovered assets of City Savings went to pay attorneys and receivers in the case. In 1985 Orin Mensik surrendered to federal authorities in Pennsylvania. He said he had been living a pauper's life on the run. A judge ordered him to complete the two to three years left on his term and tacked on an extra 30 days punishment. Mensik, an old man, said he wanted to rejoin his wife who was living in Arizona. No one ever found out where the money went. No one was ever prosecuted for the City Savings debacle, not Mensik nor any State regulators.

After all these years I still have a vivid picture in my mind of that scene in Judge Campbell"s courtroom. The scrub women, sobbing and screaming and swinging their umbrellas. Crooks! Crooks!

SLUDGE:
CHICAGO'S LIQUID GOLD

Circa 1971

I REMEMBER IT WAS *a Saturday and it must not have been in baseball season cause we were sent up to do an interview on Addison Street near Wrigley Field and it was pretty quiet around there. As was customary in those old film days we asked our man to come outside for the interview so there was no hassle about setting up lights. His name was Valentine Janicki, a trustee of the Metropolitan Sanitary District of Greater Chicago, an obscure government agency whose mission was to dispose of the city's sewage and keep the water clean. The District had a budget the size of General Motors and a reputation for corruption. In the interview Janicki told us about a new idea for the use of the black sludge which is the end product of all the raw sewage that goes through the sanitary system. Janicki said the stuff made great fertilizer and could be a boon to worn out farm land everywhere. He described the sludge as liquid gold. When the interview was over Janicki stuffed a couple of twenty dollar bills in my pocket. 'I can't take that ," I said,and slammed the bills back to him. 'We don't do business that way." " Oh I just wanted to buy you breakfast." " Give it to the crew I said." The crew was tickled to get it. Obviously my suspicions were*

aroused by Commissioner Janicki. The sludge story would go on
for several years. Somewhere along the way I was given a small
jar of the black, tar-like substance. My wife said it was real good
for our tomato plants. The story would finally end in one of the
great trials of my career.

A television news story broadcast October 12, 1971: These
barges are carrying sludge, a by product of the one and a half
billion gallons of sewage that passes through the metropolitan
Chicago area each day. Every thirty six hours four barges make
the 200 mile trip down the Illinois River to Fulton County.
Here the sludge is pumped through eleven miles of pipeline to
a holding reservoir. For a long time engineers of the Chicago
Sanitary District have claimed that this black, tar like material
is rich in Nitrogen, Potassium and Phosphorous and that it is
an excellent fertilizer when applied to the land. The Sanitary
District has purchased seven thousand acres of abandoned
strip mine land in Fulton County to prove its point. Having
run out of space in Chicago the new property will provide a
place to store the sludge. The people who live around here hope
the sludge will provide a way to reclaim thousands of acres in
the County that have been devastated by strip mining. The first
real test came when corn was planted on five acres. Part of the
land was treated with sludge, the other part not. The difference
in the crops was remarkable. Some Fulton County farmers are
still not convinced. They worry the sludge will pollute wells and
nearby lakes and streams. To prove that its main concern is
the environment the Sanitary District has turned part of the
property over to the County for use as a recreation area. And
District officials believe time will show that sludge is more of an
asset than a liability.

Another TV news story broadcast a few years later, April
23, 1974: A lot of people laughed a few years ago when
members of the Chicago Metropolitan Sanitary District

said that the end product of sewage treatment, sludge as it is called, would be a good thing to apply to land as fertilizer. One District trustee even called it liquid gold. But the District went ahead and purchased thousands of acres of abandoned strip mine property in downstate Fulton County and began transporting the sludge there. Early results were encouraging. Corn, soybeans and other grains grew much better on the treated land. Now the sludge project has been named the outstanding engineering project of 1974 by the prestigious American Society of Civil Engineers, beating out such noteworthy projects as Chicago's Sears Tower and the San Francisco's Bay Area Rapid Transit system. Sanitary District Trustees are elated. They are hopeful this new achievement will create more interest in the value of sludge and what it can do. With the current shortage of fertilizer they say farmers are making more inquiries and the Trustees themselves continue to use sludge on their lawns and gardens.

Alas, the temptations are sometimes too great in government even when the program seems worthy. Fast forward a few more years and the United States Attorney for the Northern District of Illinois, Sam Skinner, is holding a news conference. Skinner is announcing a sixty-six page indictment charging eight men in a scheme of bribery,, conspiracy, mail fraud, fraud by wire and income tax evasion. The government said that 1.2 million dollars in bribes were paid by Ingram Barge Corporation of New Orleans to obtain favorable contracts to haul sludge for the Metropolitan Sanitary District of Chicago. The no bid contracts were said to be worth an estimated forty-three million dollars. Those indicted were: two District trustees, Valentine Janicki and Chester Majewski, the District's Superintendant, Bart Lynam, an early director of the sludge project, State Representative Robert McPartlin, Franklin Weber, a consulting engineer. and Edwin Bull, a Joliet tug boat operator. Also charged were two officials of Ingram Barge, Chairman Frederick Ingram of New Orleans and his brother, Bronson of Nashville, Tennessee, President of the company

It was the largest bribery case in Illinois history. The indictments were the result of a two year investigation which Skinner said began with a phone call from a concerned citizen. But it was widely believed in political and media circles the whistle blower was a jilted secretary at the Sanitary District who knew what was going on and dropped a dime on the FBI. Robert McPartlin, accused of being an intermediary in the bribery scheme was a veteran state legislator. He was the father of nine children and a Marine veteran in the Pacific in World War II. He was not a big name in the Democratic organization. But the FBI and Justice Department lawyers hoped the threat of long prison time might force him to implicate some higher ups who were getting part of the bribe money. McPartlin wouldn't budge. Years later, before his death, Bob McParlin told friends how much the government tried to squeeze him. The feds told him if he didn't cooperate he would be sent to one of the worst prison tiers in the system where he would be repeatedly gang raped. McPartlin told this to one of his colleagues in the legislature who took him to see Dan Rostenkowski, a ranking member of the U.S. House. They all got on a plane for Washington, D.C. and had a meeting with the new President, Jimmy Carter. The President reportedly was aghast that his Justice Department would use such threatening tactics. He made a phone call and the threats against McParlin ceased.

The trial went on for weeks. The government's key witness was the bag man for Ingram barge, William Joseph Benton, a company vice president. Joe Benton, as he was known, was a scoundrel of the first order. He admitted embezzling money from his own company and bribing public officials all over the world. Often he kept some of the bribe money for himself.

He dined at the best restaurants and entertained at the best brothels. Under his deal with the federal government he was given immunity from prosecution. There would be no punishment and Joe Benton would go back to his posh nursery farm in Alabama.He was not the most trustworthy witness. But he did keep a diary with the dates and amounts of payments he made to defendants. And, for the most part, those entries jibed with other documents and testimony that came into evidence.

Frederick and Bronson Ingram were from one of the richest families in the South. Much of their defense was that they were horrified when they learned they had to pay money to get business from the Chicago Sanitary District. But they believed that's what you had to do in Chicago and they needed the sludge contract to keep their business healthy. They also presented many character witnesses. There was a light moment in the trial when golfing legend Arnold Palmer appeared in behalf of Bronson Ingram. Palmer told the jury that Ingram had been a close friend for twenty years, that they had traveled and golfed together and that he often relied on Ingram for business advice. When he was finished, Federal Judge John Grady asked the prosecutor, Gordon Nash, if he had any questions for Mr. Palmer. "I have some questions," Nash replied, "but they don't pertain to this case." The courtroom broke up. Other character witnesses included a surgeon and Professor of medicine from Tulane University and a U.S. District Court Judge from Louisiana.

When it was finally over five of the defendants were found guilty: Frederick Ingram, Valentine Janicki, Franklin Weber, Edwin Bull, and Robert McPartlin. After appeals all eventually went to jail. Three defendants, Bronson Ingram, Bart Lynam and Chester Majewski were found not guilty and went home. Former legislator Bob McPartlin was sentenced to eight years in prison. He served his time in the Federal Minimum Security

Prison in Lexingtom, Kentucky where other politicians have done time. Afterward he told friends the prison officials made his life miserable because he had used Washington clout to get in there. Frederick Ingram was sentenced to four years. After serving only fourteen months, President Jimmy Carter, a lame duck, commuted his sentence to time served. Among those who wrote letters in his behalf were Senator Howard Baker and the Roman Catholic Cardinal Archbishop of New Orleans. Representative Bob McPartlin died of cancer in 1987. He was sixty years old.

THE MAYOR OF
ROSEMONT

Circa 1972

Y OU HEAR A *lot today about people trying to manipulate the news media and shape public opinion. It's been going on forever. There's always been a need for information in fields like journalism, law enforcement or the stock market. Some might say it's far more sophisticated today because of the internet and social media. What worries me is that reporters today are getting tips and stories in e-mails, face book posts, tweets and other platforms. They aren't looking that source straight in the eye to find out if they might be lying or have some ax to grind. To be good at this was quite an art form in my day. I remember doing a series of stories years ago when I came to the conclusion that the Mafia was probably feeding stories to law enforcement to further their interests. And I believed one of the messengers or sources was a politician who was the subject of our news series, the Mayor of Rosemont, Illinois.*

In the summer of 1972 I was assigned to work with the Better Government Association and Chicago Today Newspaper on an in depth report on the Village of Rosemont and its longtime Mayor, Donald Stephens. The Better Government Association or BGA was an old Civic Watch Dog organization that frequently worked with local newspapers to uncover wrongdoing in government and politics. At the time it was headed by a hard charging former prosecutor, J. Terrence Brunner. The BGA was branching out into television. Chicago Today was the afternoon paper owned by the Chicago Tribune Corporation. I was working with four highly regarded young investigators for the BGA, Rich Samuels, William Rechtenwald, William Hood and Patrick Oster. The reporter for the paper was Greg Ramshaw. All of these young men were overachievers. Samuels was a scholar from the University of Chicago who became a top reporter at my own station and later in Public Television. Bill Rechtenwald went on to become an investigative reporter for the Tribune. Greg Ramshaw later worked for the fledgling Cable News Network in Washington. Patrick Oster became a world class journalist for newspapers and magazines and later an author,

Why was there interest in this tiny little Village just outside Chicago? A little History is needed to answer that question. Back in the 1920's gangster Al Capone and his organization were taking a lot of heat from law enforcement in Chicago. A reform mayor had been elected. So Capone moved his headquarters to the little town of Cicero on the Western border of the city. There the mob influence remained for many years after Capone's death. And it spread to other near suburbs like Elmwood Park, Schiller Park and eventually, Rosemont. Rosemont was just a neighborhood of eighty or so residents when it was incorporated in 1956. The head of the neighborhood Association, Donald Stephens, would become the village's first Mayor. Though it was small, Rosemont had a fabulous location. Chicago was building O'Hare International Airport next door. Chicago needed a small piece of Rosemont land to connect the airport to the city. Stephens negotiated this deal with Alderman Thomas Keane of the Chicago City

Council who is the subject of another story in this book, A Model Prisoner. Rosemont also had easy access to downtown Chicago by public transportation or nearby expressways. On the seamier side was nearby Manheim Road, a notorious red light and gambling district. There was also a hotel and restaurant in town called the Caravelle where mobsters liked to congregate. The mortgage on the place was held by gangsterr Sam "Mooney" Giancana who, at the time, was living in exile in Mexico. Mayor Donald Stephens and a partner purchased the Caravelle from a Giancana trust. Attesting to the mob influence in towns like Rosemont was a magazine article of the time by famed crime reporter Sandy Smith. Smith had obtained an FBI wiretap following the famous 50's national convention of La Cosa Nostra leaders held in Appalachin, New York. That meeting was busted by state police and was a great embarrassment to the wise guys. The article detailed a heated conversation between Western New York crime boss, Stefano Maggadino and Chicago"s Tony Accardo.? "You shoulda had the meeting out here. We got our own suburbs and police departments." Accardo lectured Maggadino

By 1972, when we were doing our serics, Rosemont had prospered and the mob influence had grown too. I liked the assignment. Investigators for the BGA did all the leg work. I attended some of their interviews which were conducted in police like fashion. I then produced the stories for TV. The BGA people dug up a lot of dirt on Stephens. We didn't put it all on the air or in the paper. Unlike today, in 1972 you had to be certain of the facts. Stephens seemed to be in business all over town; insurance, real estate, a car wash that was paid by the village to clean public vehicles. The police chief entertained at the Caravelle Lounge and billed the village. Stephens was a stockholder in a bank in nearby Schiller Park which was a depository of Village funds. Two trustees of the

Village had accused the Mayor of bribery. They had opposed him politically and they said Stephens wanted to get them aboard his program. Another opposing trustee started voting with the Mayor after he was offered an interest in one of the Mayor's franchise businesses. Meanwhile we reported the chief of police, a lieutenant and a sergeant were running a coin operated laundry machine business. Sources said the Mayor had an interest in the business and helped get the machines in prime village locations. Stephens denied it and he fought back. He told the Chicago Tribune the bribery charges by the two trustees and accusations of conflict of interest were all part of a political smear campaign. The local newspaper, called the Suburban Progress, sided with the Mayor. It said the BGA and the rest of us were telling only part of the story.

We continued our reporting on some of the strange things that happened in Rosemont in the past. There was the time in 1961 when a Chicago newspaper discovered that about twenty-five residents in the village were paying taxes on empty lots when there were some nice comfortable homes on the properties. The Assessor's office said the Village never submitted building permits as required by law. One of the properties was owned by Mayor Stephens, another by the Village Plumbing inspector. Mayor Stephens claimed the Assessor's Office lost the records. In 1964 State's Attorney's police raided an apartment building in Rosemont where they said a crime syndicate betting operation was doing one hundred thousand dollars worth of business every day. The owner of the building was Mayor Donald E. Stephens.

In 1968 some mail pouches containing over two million dollars worth of cash and diamonds were stolen from O'Hare Airport. The suspects and the loot were found at the Caravelle Motel in Rosemont. The thieves were from New York. Two years later they were taken out of prison to testify before a U.S. Senate crime committee investigating mail theft. They told the panel they stole a lot more than newspapers said was recovered at the time, indicating the police helped themselves to some of the stuff. About a half million dollars worth was never accounted for. When I interviewed a former police official he said many Rosemont officials and cops were wearing fancy rings and other jewelry right after that robbery. When the story about the Senate Crime Committee testimony broke, those items were not seen again.

All of the information gathered was turned over to the Cook County State's Attorney's Office, the FBI and any other agency that was interested. A grand jury was convened. But weeks and months passed and nothing ever came of our great Rosemont expose.

The State's Attorney at the time was Edward V. Hanrahan, a controversial figure, who had political problems and would lose a reelection bid that Fall to Bernard Carey, a Republican and former FBI agent. How did Stephens get through all that? I remember thinking at the time that he might be an FBI informant. The Feds were known to spend a lot of capital to protect a good source. In one of our interviews I asked the Mayor directly: Were you ever an informant for the FBI? There was a a long pause. Myself and a couple of BGA investigators waited. I remember the look in his eyes. Finally Stephens said yes, he had helped the bureau on a few raids. He said he also helped the Cook County Sheriff's Office and he mentioned the names of an FBI agent and a Sheriff's sergeant. Much later I would embrace a theory that Don Stephens was a double agent, that he fed the FBI only what the outfit guys wanted them to find out. It made some sense. I reasoned that if Stephens admitted he helped the FBI in an interview with us, and it was true, the mob would have him killed in a minute. Ten years later Stephens would be indicted on separate charges of tax fraud and bribery. In the tax case Stephens testified he relied entirely on the advice of his accountant. Unfortunately the accountant had died and could not testify. But he was found not guilty in both cases. Some veterans of the Federal Building argued that never would have happened if he was an FBI informant.

Donald Stephens served as Mayor of Rosemont for more than fifty years until his death in 2007 at the age of seventy-nine. He would become a powerhouse in Illinois politics, a confidante of three consecutive GOP Governors. He was able to raise a huge war chest of political funds from Rosemont and the surrounding township which he generously shared with favored candidates. He was also good for Rosemont, a great builder in the style of the late Mayor Richard J. Daley of Chicago. During his tenure the 18,500 seat Rosemont Horizon was built. It later became the Allstate Arena, home to DePaul basketball, Chicago Wolves hockey, Chicago Sky of the WBA and a variety of concerts. He built one of the largest convention centers in the nation.It was named for him after his death. The four thousand seat Rosemont Theater is one of the finest of the legitimate stage. All of this along a mile long strip of River Road that resembles a mini Las Vegas. The lush River Casino is just across the street in the city of DesPlaines.

Hundreds of thousands of visitors pass through Rosemont every day. It has been good for the more than four thousand village residents who live in a small gated community. Gone are the days of vacant lot tax bills. Property owners receive a $4200 tax rebate every year.

Rosemont has also been good to the Stephens family. Donald Stephens' son,Brad, is now the Mayor. He recently received a

53% increase in his salary to Two hundred sixty thousand a year. He makes more than the Mayor of Chicago. A nephew, Chris, is the two hundred fifty thousand dollar manager of the convention center. Another nephew, Donald Stephens III runs the police and fire departments. His annual salary is one hundred eighty thousand dollars.

All the world's a stage,
And all the men and women merely players;
They have their exits and their entrances,
And one man in his time plays many parts

from As You Like it
by William Shakespeare

PART II

THE CHARACTERS

ANDY MCGANN

(You can't be bothering
the President of the United States)

ANDY MCGANN WAS a Commissioner of the city of Chicago. That's the way he liked to introduce himself. Commissioner Andrew J. McGann.

He was a member of the board of the City Colleges, appointed by the late Mayor Richard J. Daley. But Commissioner was the title he preferred.

When I first saw Andy, the tears were streaming down his cheeks. He was giving a concession speech in his campaign headquarters on Ashland Avenue. Andy had just lost a squeaker to Bob Kellam in a special election for alderman of the 18th ward on Chicago's South side. It was 1977.

It was a classic Irish bloodletting that had pitted neighbors and family members against each other in that old bungalow belt neighborhood. Andy was broken hearted that night but he was no quitter.

Like most World War II and Korean War era veterans, McGann had taken off his uniform, started a business and thrown himself into community life.

He was educated at Worsham College of Mortuary Science and the Andrew J. McGann and Sons Funeral Home was started. Those who ever attended a funeral under his direction are not likely to forget him. The silver hair, the red face, the rolling thunder voice: "The bereaved will now gather with me at the head of the casket. Let us now recite the Our Father." He received many civic awards and honors but was most proud of his selection as Sir Knight-Sovereign Militia Order of Malta, one of the highest honors the Catholic Church can bestow on a layman.

Andy went on to serve ten years in the Illinois House of Representatives where he enjoyed rising to speak enthusiastically about many issues both for and against.

But my favorite story was about Andy's encounter with the White House. He told it when we were having dinner at a restaurant in Springfield, a small group of legislators and me in the early 1980's. It was a bipartisan group. Democrats and Republicans often dined together back then.

This is how Andy told the story: It was early 1961, shortly after John F. Kennedy was sworn in as President of the United States, the first Catholic to attain that high office.

We were all young Democrats then and we were riding pretty high. It was our custom, a group of my buddies and I, to get together on Saturday nights in my basement recreation room.

We'd drink some beer and play cards and talk sports. My dear Mary would make us sandwiches. And, eventually, the conversation always turned to politics.

There were stories about ringing doorbells in the precincts and marching with Jack Kennedy in Mayor Daley's torchlight parade.

The hour would grow late. And I'm sure most of us had too much beer. I'm not certain how it started exactly. We were always talking about our beloved Jack Kennedy and how thrilled we all were that he made it to the White House.

And then one night somebody said: Let's call him.

What, call the White House? Well, right away every man was in favor of it. And the enthusiasm was tremendous.

Andy, let's do it. Just call and offer our best wishes. From the guys in the 18th ward in Chicago. Just tell him we worked so hard for him and tell him he has our support in anything he does.

I mean to tell you everybody was fired up. And it soon became apparent I was the guy who was going to make the call.

So we called information and we called the White House. I don't know if they still do this today, but at that time, if you called the White House and identified yourself as an elected or appointed official, they'd put you through to a special operator.

I remember how thrilled I was that first time I heard the woman's voice: Good evening, the White House.

Good evening ma'am. This is Commissioner Andrew J. McGann of the city of Chicago. And I was wondering if I could speak for a few moments with the President?

Commissioner McGann, I'm going to connect you to Mrs. Jackson, who's an assistant to the President.

Mind you, it's near midnight on a Saturday night and I'm going to talk to an assistant to the president.

Commissioner McGann, How can I help you this evening?

Well ma'am, some of my colleagues and I were gathered here tonight and we were reminiscing about the campaign and this and that. And Mrs. Jackson, we all worked on his campaign in Chicago. And we were wondering if we could just talk to the President briefly to pledge our support and wish him all the best. And I'm sure we'd be speaking for our beloved Mayor Richard J. Daley too.

Oh, that's so thoughtful of you Mr. McGann but I'm afraid the president isn't available right now.

Just for ten seconds would he take our call?

Now the fellas are all gathered around the phone and they're making a lot of noise. We want Jack! We want Jack!

And Mrs. Jackson says: Commissioner, I'll pass your message along to the President's staff. Good Night.

So that was that. But it happened again on other Saturday nights. Someone would always yell out: Let's call Jack Kennedy and we'd be at it again. And I must say Mrs. Jackson got to know us. She was polite for awhile, but after the third or fourth call she got a little testy.

Oh please, can't we talk to our Jack for just a few minutes. We love him.

Commissioner McGann. The President cannot be disturbed. Goodbye!

The last time we did it , it was pretty late. By 1 AM all the fellas had left and I was alone in the basement cleaning up all the beer bottles. And there was a loud wrap on the door. When I opened it, I saw a big, determined-looking young man and he was holding up his credentials. United States Treasury. Secret Service.

Mr. McGann this is a warning. You have to stop calling the President of the United States.

Aw, we meant no harm. We love our dear Jack and me and the fellas just wanted to say hello.

Just the same, Mr. McGann, you have to stop calling. You can't be bothering the President of the United States.

So that ended our Saturday night phone calls to the White House. We never did get to talk to the President.

And then suddenly, on November 22, 1963, our dear Jack was shot and killed by an assassin in Dallas, Texas. God rest his sweet soul.

A Model Inmate

(Tom Keane)

THOMAS KEANE WAS a brilliant man and he had grown wealthy during his career as alderman on the Chicago City Council and political leader in his neighborhood. Mayor Daley had made him chairman of the Finance Committee and he ran it with total authority but he ran it well. Chicago, in those days, had a great credit rating.

The problem with Keane was that he wasn't very well liked. He had tiny eyes and a crooked little smile that seemed to say: "brace yourself, I'm getting ready to take you to the cleaners." If an alderman, usually an independent, had the nerve to introduce an ordinance without his approval Keane would jump to his feet and shout: "Motion to lay on the table." All in favor say aye and Daley would bang the gavel. The proposal was on the table forever, dead.

Many on the council, especially the younger ones, objected to the way he would submit the administration's finance bills on the same day they were to be voted on so no one had time to read them. They said even the Mayor was sometimes leery of his tactics. But Keane's expertise in financial affairs trumped everyone.

This talent helped Keane become a wealthy man. He was a lawyer and he was clever with real estate transactions. He had negotiated with the suburban village of Rosemont to annex property so the city would be connected to its new airport, O'Hare Field. Everyone finished in the money on that deal.

In Chicago a wealthy alderman often ends up in jail. But everyone knew that Tom Keane was too smart for that. If his dealings were not always ethical they were legal. Keane subscribed to the old Tammany Hall rule of George Washington Plunkett. Don't take a nickel from anyone. Just hand them your business card.

But, in the 1970's a new federal prosecutor took charge of the Northern District of Illinois. Big Jim Thompson was young, smart, articulate and a Republican. He was also ambitious. This combination made it easy for him to target Chicago's city hall where corruption was built into the walls. As one old reporter put it: "You can't be around the hall too long before you get hit with some falling graft."

Thompson had some bright assistant U.S. attorneys who found innovative ways to apply federal statutes to the activities of local politicians and city workers. They charged Keane with mail fraud and conspiracy in connection with his vote to have the city purchase properties in which he had a financial interest.. In 1974 he was sentenced to five years in prison. He served nearly two years of the sentence before being released. While he was away, his wife, Adeline, held his seat on the council.

On the day of Keane's release I was sent to the federal prison at Lexington, Kentucky to cover the event.

Prison officials had told us Keane was free to go any time after 6 AM. So my camera crew and I were there a few minutes early. It was a cold morning in March. We were joined by Ron Koziol, a salty veteran of the Chicago Tribune and a still photographer from one of the wire services.

It was still dark out when the front door of the institution opened and the old alderman appeared in hat and overcoat.

He made his way quickly the short distance to a waiting station wagon driven by his wife. The lights went on, the cameras rolled and flashed. "Alderman Keane, how does it feel to be a free man? What will you do now, alderman? But the questions were ignored and he was gone. Koziol turned to me and said: You know the guy never had any PR sense." Such a long trip for about fifteen seconds of film.

Later I interviewed a prison employee who ran the sewage treatment plant where Keane had worked. "He was the best employee I ever had," he said. "He kept perfect records and even docked fellow inmates if they were even five minutes late for work." But he accepted none of the token pay and asked that it be given to the men.

Years later the Supreme court found part of the mail fraud statute, which convicted Keane, to be unconstitutional. However, the court denied Keane's request to have his record expunged.

Alderman Keane died in 1996 at the age of ninety.

BOBBY RUSH

E'S STILL A congressman as I write this but he doesn't look too good when I see him on television. He's had some health issues. And he's had some ethical problems like many other poor people in our history who've been elected to public office; the usual stuff, bills not paid, money unaccounted for.

But when I first met Bobby Rush he was a young dude with a mission, Minister of Defense for the Black Panther Party. The Panthers were a radical group composed of young black men who were fed up with the system and how it treated their people.

They did some good things too. They ran a bus to the Pontiac State prison, a hundred miles to the Southwest of Chicago. I rode on it one time with a camera crew. It was a good story. Mostly it was poor mothers getting a chance to visit their sons who were incarcerated far from Chicago. It was a trip they couldn't afford to make on their own. I got to know some of the Panthers although they were always suspicious of a white guy. They needed the media.

The Panthers really hated the cops, calling them pigs all the time. The police had killed Panther leader Fred Hampton in a raid on his West side apartment. They found guns there. But the fire power was pretty one sided favoring the police. The Panthers said Hampton had been murdered.

Bobby Rush appeared on our noon TV news the next day. Every other word was pig. The phone switchboard lit up with irate viewers. The controversy went on and on. Mayor Daley dumped the incumbent states attorney from the Democratic ticket. His name was Edward Hanrahan and he had authorized the Panther raid.

A year later I was assigned to a West side church where the Panthers were marking the first anniversary of Hampton's death. My cameraman, who may have been suffering combat fatigue, didn't want to go. I too felt a little uncomfortable.

The church was dark and the crew complained they'd have to put up lights. One of the party officials told me there was going to be a short service and then a film of Fred Hampton's life would be shown. The program would begin shortly. I told the crew to standby and then took a seat in a pew half way up toward the altar.

Right from the start I noticed the Panther security guys prowling the aisles. They all seemed to focus on me. The scary part was I knew they were all packing heat. The sad thing was these young Panthers believed the cops were out to kill them all. And they were probably right about that. The tension was broken a little when the service started and we filmed it. We looked like we were there to do a real job. But the service was brief and then they announced the start of the film. That's when all the lights went out. The only light came from the picture projected on the screen in front of the church. The crew and I sat in separate pews. The young Panther bodyguards got more active. They kept eyeballing me. Then it got worse. At that moment our courier arrived to pick up film. This was a real live Chicago cop and he was probably armed. Dressed in a light tan raincoat he came swaggering up to me. "Pete, have you got any film to send back?" I told him to sit down quietly. It would be a little while before we could ship.

Now the security guys seemed really dangerous. They kept hovering around, hands in their pockets. The film on Fred Hampton's life went on and on. When it ended the lights came on. I felt the need to do something that might help avoid violence. I turned and saw Bobby Rush at the rear of the church. That was the answer. Go see Bobby. I hurried back but this further alarmed the bodyguards. They rushed at me from all directions. But I was able to get to Bobby first. I reached out and Bobby gave me a great big soul handshake. "Hey Pete, what's happening." In that brief moment peace was at hand. Everything was cool after that.

"BULL JIVE"

HIS NAME WAS James Taylor, State Representative James Taylor who represented a district in Chicago's South side black belt. He was the committeeman or political boss of the sixteenth ward. He was born in Arkansas and came to Chicago in his youth. A big tough fellow, he was a heavyweight boxer before he joined the Democratic Machine and got a job on the city payroll as a sanitation worker.

Later he became better known as Jimmy "Bull Jive" Taylor. The "Bull Jive" part came from a quote which he gave to Chicago newspaper columnist Mike Royko. Royko had been approached by two enterprising young black women who wanted to open a beauty parlor in the sixteenth ward. They needed zoning approval from ward boss Taylor and sought a meeting with him. According to the women Taylor was agreeable to the project if they would provide some sexual favors. The ladies were shocked and went to Royko with their story.

News people frequently receive such information about politicians and celebrities. But the story is often difficult to confirm. The politician will deny it and you're left with a he said she said tale. Royko dutifully made the call to Representative Taylor. To his surprise and delight Jimmy admitted he met with the women and yes, he did ask for sex. "But I was just bull jivin em," Jimmy proclaimed. This was the making of a great Royko column and Jimmy's middle name became "Bull Jive."

I liked Jimmy Taylor. He was a loyal Democratic machine guy. There was never a deviation. He held good jobs, mostly as a garbage man. All his precinct captains were with the Sanitation Department. And when Jimmy got elected to the legislature, he began collecting two paychecks, one from the city and one from the state. Life was good.

When Representative Taylor arrived in Springfield he was seated in one of the upper back rows in the house chamber. His seat mates were downstate, redneck Democrats whose districts were not far from the Mason-Dixon line. When party leaders asked Jimmy if he wanted to move to a more integrated section of the chamber, Jimmy said he would stay put. Gradually he made friends with the downstaters. He regaled the boys with stories of his boxing days and life in Chicago's South side black neighborhood. Soon Representative Taylor was voting to fund corn detaseling bills in Southern Illinois. The country boys began supporting Chicago welfare programs.

Legislative bodies, like the schools, are the front lines of integration. People have to sit together every day. They talk and get to know each other, know their problems, their good times and bad times. Some of them may come to like each other. There's even a willingness to cooperate. That's what happened to Jimmy Taylor in the legislature.

When Jane Byrne went up against the organization in 1979 and got elected Mayor, Jimmy Taylor made peace with Jane and got an upper five figure job as her deputy chief of staff. The end came for Jimmy four years later when Harold Washington beat Byrne and Richard M. Daley for Mayor. Jimmy was a long time enemy of the new mayor. Harold stripped him of his patronage and knocked him out of politics. When he died in 1999 at the age of sixty-nine, Bull Jive was driving a taxi cab.

As an old Tammany Hall boss once said: 'Politics ain't bean bag.' "

EPTON BEFORE IT'S TOO LATE

(Excerpted from the book CAMPAIGN! The 1983 Election that Rocked Chicago)

"THE TROUBLE WITH Bernie Epton is that he's had a headache for thirty years." The comment was made by a colleague in jest, but if you saw Epton in the Illinois House of Representatives, leaning back in his big leather chair, frequently with a hot white towel covering his head, you knew there was something to it.

Once he went down, passed out right there on the house floor. Worried colleagues rushed to his side. One of them was Representative Bruce Douglas, a dentist from Chicago "Get that dentist out of here," Bernie gasped as he came around. "I don't need a dentist." Bernie was ok then, just a fainting spell, but the headaches continued. (this happened between 1971 and 1975. Douglas was in the 77th and 78th general assemblies)

The headaches may have come from the war. Bernie had enlisted in the Army Air Corps in 1942 and rose to the rank of captain. He flew twenty five bombing missions over Germany and was awarded two distinguished flying crosses. General Doolittle awarded him a personal citation. There were many war heroes serving with Bernie Epton in the Illinois house in the 1970's, including a medal of honor winner, Clyde Choate of Anna, Illinois.

Bernie Epton came home from the war with a beautiful English bride,Audrey. They settled in Hyde Park near the University of Chicago and had four children. Hyde Park was the only integrated community in Chicago for many years after the war. Bernie's kids went to public schools.

Epton established a successful law practice with many leading insurance companies as clients. He stood over six feet, a neat beard offset his bald head. He was well tailored. He could have been a professor at the University of Chicago or a Rabbii. He was known for his extra dry wit and gained a reputation as a progressive Republican who supported civil rights issues and gave generously to African-American causes.

Bernie had a flare for drama. In 1961 he tried to put together a deal to buy the Chicago White Sox. Epton and his partner, comedian Danny Thomas, reportedly made an offer to buy a majority of the club's stock for 4.8 million dollars. But the proposal was rejected.

And then, in 1983, he decided to run for mayor of Chicago. That's when things started to go down hill for Bernie Epton. He would be called a racist, he would become embittered, attack the news media and eventually die of a broken heart.

It really wasn't such a bad idea to begin with. A Republican hadn't been elected mayor of Chicago since the 1920's. The Democratic machine was in disarray since the death of Richard J. Daley in 1976. The current Mayor, Jane Byrne, was a maverick who had defeated the Democratic organization but now had her own political liabilities. So Bernie took the plunge in the hope that he might be a viable alternative to the warring Democrats.

Politics was changing when Bernie Epton ran for Mayor.

The news media was out of control. CNN had begun twenty-four-hour news coverage. British-style journalism invaded the United States and the tabloid news shows were firing up. The networks followed with cheap documentaries. The "in your face" style was in vogue, not just in the media, but in politics and business. There was profit to be made in TV news . No longer would it be public service.

Political handling and consulting was a growth industry. The crafty handlers knew what the media wanted, not campaign position papers, but confrontation. Some of those bozos came to town and found their way to the Epton campaign, after the heated Democratic primary.

In the beginning of the campaign of 1983 Bernie Epton wasn't much more than an afterthought. He was the Republican candidate for mayor. That title was one that comedian Rodney Dangerfield would have some fun with. When President Ronald Reagan came to Chicago, Epton was given a back seat in the banquet hall.

But in the final days of the primary campaign something happened. There were three Democratic candidates. Jane Byrne, the Incumbent Mayor, Richard M. Daley, the Cook County State's Attorney and son of the late Mayor, and Harold Washington, an African American congressman. Daley had been the early favorite but toward the end, the Byrne camp convinced white ethnics that a vote for Daley was a vote for Washington. Byrne and Daley split the white vote. Washington took the black vote and a good portion of the white independent/liberal vote to claim a stunning upset.

Now Bernie Epton was no longer an afterthought. He was the GOP candidate for Mayor of Chicago. And for many Chicagoans he now was the white candidate. Harold Washington had vowed to dismantle the Democratic machine so many white Democrats went to work for Epton. Bernie began appearing at events sponsored by these ward organizations. He surely was thrilled as the crowds shouted: Bernie! Bernie! Bernie!. Or were they really shouting: White guy! Wwhite guy! White guy!

Bernie Epton got caught up in a racial campaign in a city divided by race since its inception. The media would label him a racist. African Americans called him a racist and a clown. It didn't help matters when his political handlers created the campaign slogan: Epton before it's too late.

I'm standing on a street corner on the near Northwest side of Chicago when I see Bernie Epton approaching me.. He had just finished a news conference about his plans to improve housing and schools. There must be close to two hundred photographers and reporters dispersing and now here's Bernie coming toward me. It was early April and still overcoat cold in Chicago. Bernie was running for Mayor.

Can you believe it? A Jewish Republican from the intellectual neighborhood around the University of Chicago and he's a nose hair away from winning the election just a couple of weeks away.

Now he's walking my way and I'm a little nervous cause there's still a lot of media around and I'm trying to figure out what he wants with me.

The news media had come from all over the world to cover this wild campaign. Just that morning a reporter from Australia rushed up to me: Is he really as big a racist as they make him out to be? I told him I didn't think so but by this time I wasn't sure what was going on. Bernie was being portrayed as a racist, there was no doubt about that. It didn't help that his campaign had come up with that nasty slogan: EPTON, BEFORE IT'S TOO LATE. What the hell was that all about? Most African Americans and many others took it to mean: EPTON, BEFORE IT'S TOO LATE AND CHICAGO HAS A BLACK MAYOR.

Now Bernie was in front of me:

Pete, how much money do you make?

What?

I want to know how much you make. Are you under a contract to NBC?

Bernie, what the hell are you talking about? Why are you asking me this?

Peter, I'm going to win this election and I want to hire you as my press secretary. The city can't afford to pay you what NBC is paying you but I'll make up the difference from my own pocket. If I get elected I've got to have people around me I can trust and I think you're that type of person.

Bernie, I've got six kids. Some of them are still in high school. I'd have to move into the city.. There's no way I could do this. And you shouldn't be making an offer like this today.. I'm a reporter covering your campaign. It's a conflict of interest. I said that last part loud because several reporters were moving close to us, all of them on the eario.

It's a good thing I didn't quit my job cause Bernie lost that election. During the campaign someone stole his medical records and they were duly publicized in the papers and on TV. Bernie had one time sought help for depression brought on by chronic headaches and stomach problems. When I interviewed him on election night he was pretty upset. "They're just scum," he said of the news media.

He never got over that election. " He was a bitter and broken man," his brother Jerry said. "From the night of the election on there wasn't much communication between us. And we had been very close. I didn't see him much in Florida after that."

In 1987 when Harold Washington was completing his

tumultuous first term, The New York Times News Service speculated about a Republican candidate for Mayor of Chicago but made no mention of Epton who had come so close to defeating Harold. Author Thomas Landess called Epton to see if he was going to run again. As caustic as ever Epton told him: "Sure, I've just been drafted by a citizens committee but I probably won't be endorsed by the Republican Party." When asked if the press knew he had been drafted Epton replied, "Of course they knew, I told them I've already been booked on a couple of talk shows."

A blue ribbon committee of Republicans, recommended Donald Haider to be the party's candidate for Mayor. Haider was a former Northwestern University business professor. Still Epton said he would run in the primary. But the Epton campaign had not been astute in filing its petitions. The Chicago Democratic machine has always had Draconian rules for becoming a candidate making it easy to get rid of unwanted strangers seeking office. A disgruntled Republican from the eleventh ward, who said the Epton campaign owed him money from four years earlier, filed a challenge to Epton's petitions. It turned out the campaign had not filed enough extra signatures to offset faulty ones and the Board of Elections Commissioners ruled that Bernard Epton was disqualified from the primary election. Bernie took it graciously and decided not to fight it. He said the Board of Elections was right in its decision. Then he disappeared from the political scene.

In December Bernie and his wife of forty-three years, Audrey, went to visit their son Jeff and his family in Ann Arbor, Michigan. On the morning of the thirteenth Audrey tried to awaken her husband but he was unresponsive. She called the paramedics who tried to revive him but he was gone. Bernie Epton was sixty-six years old. He died less than three weeks after the death his old rival, Harold Washington.

In the Tribune obituary Lieutenant Governor George Ryan said Bernie had told him he had a private breakfast meeting with Mayor Washington. "Bernie said the mayor had asked that he serve on some city commission. I think it was a way the mayor could say publicly how much he respected Bernie. One of the biggest regrets Bernie had was the label of racist," Ryan said. "Nothing he ever did, either in private or public, was racist and that label really bothered him."

The cause of Epton's death was an apparent hear attack. His son Jeff says he died of a broken heart. "My father was angry and bitter after that election and then just sad until his life ended. I had many disputes with my father but he was the most important figure in my life. I have more of him in me than anyone else."

Jeff Epton says Harold Washington told some people privately that all the racial stuff during the campaign wasn't Bernie. He said Bernie had been his friend.

OTTO KERNER

H E WAS SITTING alone in the Eastern Airlines waiting
area in the Lexington, Kentucky airport. He had just
been released from prison and he was going home to
Chicago to begin the rest of his life.

He was leaving early, having served only seven months of a
three year sentence for bribery, conspiracy, perjury and various
other charges. In all there were seventeen counts against him.
He was found guilty on all of them. The early release was
because he had been diagnosed with lung cancer. No one had
come to pick him up and he took a cab to the airport.

He was a free man now but he looked pretty lonely sitting
there in the waiting area. The other passengers read their
papers. They paid little attention to this sixty-five year old man
who sat amongst them staring straight ahead.

His name was Otto Kerner Jr., most recently a Justice of the
United States Court of Appeals, Seventh Circuit. He had the
distinction of being the first judge to be convicted of a crime in
the entire history of the federal judiciary.

I had covered his trial which lasted seven weeks in early
1973. Kerner had been accused of receiving stock in race tracks
in return for granting favorable racing dates through the state
racing board. It was long and complicated but the bottom
line was the Governor received the money. And a jury found
him guilty. Politicians have never fared well in the Federal
Courthouse of Chicago.

At the time he had vowed to appeal the verdict. "I have been in many battles in my life where life itself was at stake. This battle is even more important than life itself because it involves my reputation and my honor." But the appeals failed. Kerner had to resign from the bench and go to prison. He lost his pension. Yet he always maintained his innocence saying he had committed an indiscretion not a crime.

Otto Kerner had been educated at the best schools, Brown University, Cambridge in England, Northwestern Law. He had risen to to the rank of Major General after fighting in North Africa and Sicily in World War II. He had been a Judge and a U.S. Attorney and the Governor of Illinois. In the 1960's President Johnson asked him to study the causes of urban riots in some of our great cities. The Kerner Commission reported that America was divided into two societies, one black and one white, and that years of bigotry and deprivation against blacks was the cause of this strife.

In the airport that day in Kentucky he had lost everything. Yet he sat straight, the angular handsome face with the distinct blue eyes staring straight forward. I realized that my camera crew and I were on the same flight. The camera crew, by virtue of their union contract, sat in the first class cabin. I asked Kerner if I could join him in coach and he said it would be OK. He knew me from the trial and I had written him in prison asking for an interview. He wrote back declining. He didn't think it would sit well with his keepers.

We began a conversation that would last through a stop at Indianapolis and on into Chicago. He was in an upbeat mood and very cordial. I supposed it was because he had regained his freedom after many months and was returning home to a beautiful wife and two devoted adult children, Anton and Helena, who had stood by him and never missed a day of his trial.

We talked current politics. Kerner seemed amused by the controversial new Democratic Governor of Illinois, Dan Walker, and his war with the old boss of Chicago Mayor Richard J. Daley. (Walker himself would do jail time for an offense that happened after he left office.)

In those days many people smoked cigarettes and smoking was allowed on airplanes. I didn't dare light up because of the Governor's cancer. To my surprise, within a short time Kerner pulled out a pack of Trues and offered me one. "But sir, you've been diagnosed with lung cancer," I objected. He told me it had been caught early and everything was going to be OK. So we smoked.

Then a flight attendant appeared and offered us drinks. I wanted to buy him one. But he wouldn't allow it, explaining that, during his prison stay, he wasn't allowed to have money. So Otto Kerner bought me a drink.

The Lexington, Kentucky Federal Prison was not not a hard, maximum security place. The inmates lived in dormitories. Still, as Kerner told me, you can't go anywhere, your freedom is gone. He spent some of his time teaching other inmates English and this was good.

I asked him if prison was a pretty tough go and he seemed a little surprised. "Tough? No this wasn't tough. I was at the Kasserine Pass in Africa in 1943. That was really tough. This was nothing compared to that." [1]

At some point I asked if I could get my camera crew in first

---

1   One thousand Americans were killed in the battle of the Kasserine Pass in Africa when German Field Marshal Erwin Rommel broke through their lines. Americans had to withdraw and leave most of their equipment behind. It was a major defeat for the allies.

class and record an interview with him. He declined. He told me I could use anything in our conversation but he wasn't up to going on camera.

When we arrived at O'Hare in Chicago I walked down the ramp with him into a mob of news media in full feeding frenzy mode. We shook hands and he waded into the crowd. He walked slowly with military bearing, eyes straight ahead. He answered no questions. I went on the ten o'clock news with Floyd Kalber that night and shared my experience.

Kerner underwent surgery and chemotherapy for lung cancer. He would die at the age of sixty-seven in a little over a year. But during the time he had left he traveled and made speeches urging reform of the nation's prisons.

Some years after Kerner's death United States District Court Judge Abraham Lincoln Marovitz gave me a letter he had sent to Kerner right after he entered prison.

Judge Abe Marovitz was one of the great Chicago characters of the twentieth century.

He was a son of Jewish immigrants from Lithuania. He was a close personal friend of Mayor Richard J. Daley. Judge Abe always delighted in telling the story of how his mother decided on his name, Abraham Lincoln. She had seen pictures of Lincoln wearing a beard and she read that he was shot in the temple. Her conclusion was that Lincoln had been a famous Rabbi. So, when she married and had her first son, she named him for the slain President. This is the letter Judge Abe sent to his friend, Otto kerner:

July 31, 1974

Otto Kerner Esq.
Federal Correctional Institution
Room 104
Lexington, Kentucky

My Dear Friend Otto:

I think you should know that in the last few days you have been the topic of more conversations among different kinds of persons and groups with whom I come in contact, than any other fellow around our community. And Otto, this is the truth- not a single one has failed to say that they thought you " got a bad deal."

I don't know how much comfort that gives you, but it's evident to me that there are a lot of people in this town who have not forgotten the many worthwhile and constructive things you did in your community and your political life. Was it Shakespeare who said, "the evil one does lives after them, but the good is often interred in their bones." That certainly is not true in your case, Otto- the people I have talked to have invariably accentuated the positive things in your life and attributed your trouble to a case of bad judgement. I cannot quarrel with that and I guess neither can you.

I am sure you will be hearing from a lot of friends and it would be unreasonable for us to expect any acknowledgements or replies- at least I think so,—so you do not have to bother acknowledging this note. I just wanted to be sure that that you knew that I still think you are a great guy and I am hoping and praying that you will be able to discipline yourself to the extent that this experience will leave you with a minimal, if any, of scarring. I know you will make yourself useful to others- and that you will keep busy-that's the best therapy in the world.

I went to the Synagogue today to recite the Kaddish prayer in memory of my beloved and Saintly mother. It was the anniversary of her death today and I said a prayer for you and for your mother, asking the Good Lord to keep her strong and enjoy her for some years more. I am confident that Tony and Helena will continue to be strong too. those are three very good reasons, none better,— your mother and those two wonderful kids that should motivate you to make the very best of a bad situation.

You will be in my thoughts and prayers and my secretary, Aileen, who came to me after Mickey retired, asked if she could say "Me too." Of, course I will add one for my beloved Mickey who, I am sure, would want to say that in capital letters.

God Bless.

Cordially,
Your friend Abe

HOFFA

IT WAS A couple of days before Christmas in 1971. We were on a plane from Chicago to St. Louis. I was with Ted Elbert, an NBC network producer and our camera crew. On the same flight was a crew from CBS along with their reporter, Michele Clark, the first African American woman to become a network correspondent. I knew Michele when she was a local reporter in Chicago. I don't think I ever met a nicer person in this crazy business.[2]

As friendly competitors, we all dined together at a nice restaurant overlooking the St. Louis arch. Everyone was excited about our assignment the next day. Jimmy Hoffa was being released from federal prison and would reunite with family at the home of a daughter in the St. Louis suburb of Glendale.

I had seen Hoffa interviewed by NBC's David Brinkley one time. As Brinkley fired questions about union corruption Hoffa

---

2   Michele Clark died a year later in the crash of A United Airlines plane near Midway Airport. She had been in the news as an eight year old child in 1951 when her family tried to move into the all white working class suburb of Cicero. Rioters burned their apartment and the family piano.

kept saying he had to protect his truck drivers from the dangers of the jungle where they worked.

Hoffa had served nearly five years of a thirteen year sentence for jury tampering and misuse of union pension money. Jimmy got jammed up making loans to mob guys. Then Attorney General Bobby Kennedy had been on Hoffa's tail for years and finally nailed him. But now Kennedy was dead and Richard Nixon was President. The Teamsters had supported him in 1968 and he wanted their support for his reelection campaign of 1972. And Hoffa had supported Nixon against Jack Kennedy in 1960 cause he hated the Kennedys.

The Nixon commutation deal prohibited Hoffa from any union activity for nine years. But on this day Hoffa was happy to be back with family in St. Louis. His wife, Josephine, had recently suffered a heart attack.

So here we all were, a media circus of maybe sixty or seventy people camped out in this nice little suburb in front of Hoffa's daughter's house. It's Christmas eve and many of us were anxious to get home. They needed to get rid of this media mob. Hoffa did the right thing. He came out on the front steps and talked to us. The cameras rolled and they clicked and flashed.

I remember Jimmy talking about his time in prison. He said he didn't like the idea of first offenders being thrown into prisons with the type of people they never knew existed. But he said he didn't hold a grudge cause that wouldn't solve anything.

Suddenly I heard noises, a commotion. Jimmy saw it first because he was looking out at the photographers. I could see the excitement in his eyes. All the reporters turned to see two male photographers trading punches and shouting. One of them was a big cameraman named Luther who worked for CBS. The other was a still photographer from a newspaper or wire service. They had been jockeying for position and it blew up.

In those days there was a lot of animosity between print people and television people who had invaded their turf. I turned to Hoffa and he was laughing and enjoying the show.

The fight was broken up but that pretty much ended the impromptu news conference. What I remember most was Hoffa's reaction to the fist fight, him getting a big kick out of it. I'm sure he was involved in many during his early union career.

The good times didn't last long for Hoffa. In July of 1975 Jimmy disappeared. He had been making plans to get back in the Teamsters Union. The outfit guys didn't want that. They were very happy with his replacement, Frank Fitzsimmons. So they downsized Jimmy, put him away somewhere, never to be found. The usual suspects are all dead now. It's one of the great unsolved murder cases of the 20th century.

Many years later in Chicago I was introduced to the son, Jimmy Hoffa Junior, who at this writing was still head of the Teamsters Union. I told him the story about the skirmish in St. Louis and his father's reaction. The younger Hoffa roared with laughter. " Yeah, that was my dad. He loved a good fight."

LUNCH with
SID LUCKMAN

Circa 1994

I HAD LUNCH WITH Sid Luckman one day when the famed quarterback was near the end of his life. On this day he was still in great form.

Jimmy Strong, the retired Chicago Tribune writer and I were going to have lunch with Steve Neal who wrote politics for the Sun Times. Steve called to say he had invited Irv Kupcinet who presided over Kup's Column, a celebrity gossip column that had become an institution in Chicago along with its author. Steve would invite Kup occasionally to our lunches. He was approaching the age of ninety and, while still writing his column, there weren't many people alive who he knew. So we all ended up at a back table at Gene and Georgetti's.[3]

When Kup arrived he said he hoped we didn't mind, that he had invited Sid Luckman to join us. I almost fell off my chair. Luckman was my boyhood hero. I had his football card. It was really something when he arrived. He was led over to the table by his uniformed chauffeur. Kup made the introductions. Then

---

3   A legendary Chicago steak house

the chauffeur stepped in and told us that Mr. Luckman wanted to present us with some gifts. He gave us each a beautiful tie. He also gave us some costume jewelry for our wives or girl friends. When I got home that day my wife informed me the jewelry was high end stuff.

So here we are sitting with this football legend. He had been an All American at Columbia and finished third for the Heisman Trophy in 1938. During his career the Chicago Bears played in five NFL championship games and won four of them. Sid would later be inducted into the pro football hall of Fame.

On the day of our lunch Sid told us how he came to become a Chicago Bear. It wasn't in the cards at first. After graduation from Columbia he married his sweetheart Estelle. She came from a prominent Jewish family. Her father owned a trucking company. The newlyweds set up housekeeping in a flat in Brooklyn. "I really thought I'd be working for my in laws," Sid said, "but then George Halas, the founder and coach of the Chicago Bears, knocked on our door." This is how he described the Halas visit.

"George Halas was a very powerful and convincing man. My wife, Estelle, was taken with him as soon as he entered the apartment. He wanted me to play quarterback for the Chicago Bears and inaugurate the T Formation backfield. He said the pay wouldn't be all that great, between five and six thousand dollars a year. But there would be income from off season work endorsing products, selling cars or working with other local businesses. Estelle was enthusiastic. She was looking starry eyed at Halas. But I'm thinking, what am I gonna tell her father, that I'm gonna support my new wife on five grand a year as a football player? "Sid, why not give it a shot," Estelle said. So I signed with the Chicago Bears and it turned out to be a very successful arrangement."

Sid Luckman probably made more money in business than

he ever did as a player for the Chicago Bears in the 1940's. He became friends with A.N. Pritzker, one of the founders of a family business empire that would one day own the Hyatt Hotel chain and is still a rich and powerful business today. In later years Luckman and the Pritzker family would make an offer to buy the Chicago Bears. At lunch that day Sid would tell us about the time Mr. Pritzker introduced him to a movie star.

"I remember it was a weekend in November and we were playing the Los Angeles Rams that Sunday. On Saturday I got a call from Mr. Pritzker. He wanted me to come to a cocktail party that night. He wanted me to meet some of his friends who were in town from California. I declined telling him that Coach Halas had placed us on strict curfew the night before any game. But Mr. Pritzker persisted. He said it would mean a lot to him and I could leave early. You have to understand the man had been very kind to me and helped me in business. So I agreed to show up at the party for a little while.

It was quite a lavish affair. I was introduced to many Hollywood types including a beautiful young actress named Ava Gardner who was just beginning her career. At one point Mr. Pritzker pulled me aside and asked if I could get him six tickets for some West Coast friends who wanted to see the Rams play the next day. In those days the players got a couple of tickets to each game. If you needed more tickets you had to talk to the coach. I told Mr. Pritzker I'd be in big trouble with Coach Halas if I called and told him I was out. Again, he asked for a special favor and I complied. As expected, when I called the coach, he was irate. What the hell are you doing out? He gave me a royal chewing out with all the colorful language for which he was known. But he said the tickets would be there and closed by telling me to get my ass in bed. I passed this along to Mr. Pritzker and prepared to leave. Then it happened.

Ava Gardner saw me saying goodbye and came over. She

was planning to leave herself and would I mind giving her a ride to her hotel? Would I mind? She was gorgeous. I was a little nervous though. I had a decent car, a Cadillac convertible that some dealer had me driving. So I took Miss Gardner to her hotel. I remember it was a beautiful night. We had the top down. And then it started to snow very lightly. She got very excited cause she had never seen snow before. I think she was an Italian girl who grew up in the South and then moved to California to be in the movies. It was her first encounter with snow. A couple of days later I received the most beautiful telegram. You are the nicest gentleman I've ever met, a real man's man. Thanks for the ride. Ava Gardner." I felt like a million dollars."

At this point I was on the edge of my chair. But that was the end of Sid's story, almost the end.

"Oh yeah, about a month later I found out who really sent that telegram. It wasn't Ava. Kup confessed that he had sent it. One of his tipsters, and he had hundreds of them, had called to report Ava Gardner and Sid Luckman leaving the Pritzker party together.

Kup never used the item. After all I was a married man. But he couldn't resist sending that telegram."

Sid Luckman and Irv Kupcinet were gentlemen of the old style. I still have the tie Sid gave me that day. There are two small labels on the back. One says: Pure Silk, Valentino, Pietro, Paris, Rome, Beverly Hills. The other one says: Custom made for a friend of Sid Luckman. I wonder if one of my descendants will find it some day many years hence and bring it to Antiques Road Show. And one of the experts will authenticate it and explain who these people were.

CROSSING the RHINE

BEFORE I BEGAN my career in the news business I taught school for a year. It was the toughest job I ever had and to this day I have the greatest admiration for school teachers.

It was 1962 and I was at Genesee- Humboldt Junior High School in Buffalo, New York teaching seventh grade English and Social Studies. When the final bell rang each day I was in the parking lot before most of the kids.

I became friends with the man across the hall, Russ Osborn, a math teacher. We had the same free period in mid morning and had coffee each day for the better part of an hour in the teachers room.

Russ was older than I. I'd say he was thirty-eight or forty at that time but he seemed like a father figure to me. He was older and wiser I'm sure because he was in World War II at a very young age.

We had many discussions that year during those free periods. I know it was a lot about world affairs and life in general. I can't remember the specifics. What I can't forget is the one time he talked about the war.

Russ had a famous father, Alex Osborn, who was one of the founders of the great advertising agency, BBD&O, Benton, Barton, Durstine and Osborn. Alex Osborn liked to put creative people in a room together and let them bounce ideas around.

The practice was called "brainstorming," a popular concept in business back in the 1950's. New York was awash in ad agencies and creative ideas in those days.

Russ told me his dad was a great Buffalo booster and insisted on raising his family there. He ran a Buffalo office and later commuted by air five hundred miles to New York where he helped save the business during the Great Depression.

Russ had gone through some changes in his life after the war. He had earned a law degree and went to work in a law firm. But the business didn't agree with him. He wanted something more contributive and so he took to teaching seventh graders math. He also took his young family across the Niagara River to Canada to live, a half hour commute to our school.

Russ Osborn crossed the Rhine River in a glider plane. He had enlisted in the Army in his early career as a student at Colgate University where he had excelled as a soccer player.

I knew a little about World War II from movies I had seen as a boy. And our neighborhood, like so many others, had a a few returning veterans. The kids idolized these returning heroes.

I was still young and naive in 1962 and I remember being quite surprised when Russ Osborn told me he had been with a platoon of armed men in a glider heading for combat in Germany. A glider? How could that be? A glider was something you bought at the hobby store, put together with glue and flew in the back yard.

Russ assured me there were big gliders in the war, thousands of them. They carried troops and even small artillery pieces. I asked Russ if he was nervous on that flight. His reply surprised me. He said he had fallen asleep. It wasn't unusual. He had some type of condition. Whenever he became nervous or excited he would fall asleep. This would happen often before an important soccer game.

So when he crossed the Rhine River in a Horsa Glider, Russ

Osborn, the young college student was asleep. He would have a
rude awakening. And he would describe it to me in vivid detail
so many years later in a teachers break room in Buffalo, New
York.

"It was total chaos when we landed," Russ said. "Men were
separated from their units. Bullets were flying everywhere.
There was machine gun and mortar fire. Much of it came from
a nearby woods. Soon we found out it was our own men firing
at us, confused as we were. At one point I made a run to find
some cover from the withering fire. I came upon a Volkswagon
car, overturned and abandoned in a clearing in the middle of
World War II. I dove under it and found a little relief. Then
I heard this sucking noise. I rolled over and next to me was a
dead man with his face blown away. And there was this sucking
noise. Chaos, I thought, chaos."

That was the end of his story. I think the bell must have rung.
Russ and I had coffee after that but he never talked about the
war again. I left town the next year and never kept in touch with
Russ Osborn.

Over my life I would read many books and see many films
about World War II, all depicting the carnage and mayhem. I
remember the closing scene of the great director David Lean's
film, Bridge on the River Kwai; the British doctor looking down
on the scene of two allied soldiers trying to kill each other, the
blowing of the bridge and the Japanese commander committing
hary cary. "Madness!," the doctor repeats, "madness!"

Later would come the Viet Nam war and the heart of
darkness, and the Middle East.

Wasn't it Pope John XXIII who said: " War is and remains
the greatest evil?" We still love and practice it today. As I grow
oldI find myself thinking more and more of Russ Osborn, a
young man crossing the Rhine River in a glider plane, and his
tale of chaos and madness.

CHICK MCCUEN

SOMEWHERE IN FRANCE on a cold New Years eve in 1944 two young American soldiers sneak out of their encampment on a mission that has nothing to do with World War II. They are looking for a place to get a drink and to celebrate. One of the men, Sergeant Ackerman has just received word that his wife, back home in New York City has given birth to a son, their first child. His companion, Charles McCuen, a reporter for the Armed Forces radio network, has been covering the movements of General George Patton's Third Army through Europe. McCuen has convinced Ackerman they need to get out and proclaim the birth of his son.

They entered a small French village which was very dark. After awhile they came upon a house that might have served as a tavern or Inn. They rapped hard on the door. No response. They rapped some more. Finally the two soldiers saw a light go on at the back. A little old man opened the door a crack. The man spoke a little English. The GI's had picked up a little French. They managed to communicate to the man that Ackerman was a new father who wanted to celebrate. The man invited them in.

More lights in the house went on. Soon other members of the family appeared. Someone went and invited neighbors in. Wine and spirits and holiday foods that had been hidden from the Germans were all brought out on the table. There was music and

dancing and toasting of the new son of Ackerman. World War II
was coming to a close. But it wasn't over yet. Many men would
still die as the allies drove into Germany. Within a short time
after that party in the French countryside, Sergeant Ackerman
of New York would lose his life in combat. The memory of that
New Years Eve party would stay with Charles McCuen as would
a perennial mission to find Ackerman's son.

After the war Chick worked in radio in Iowa and then
got hired at WCCO-TV in Minneapolis where he became a
pioneering news director and anchorman. In 1961 he joined the
staff of NBC News in Chicago and later became the Springfield
reporter where he covered the state legislature. That's when I
first met Chick. Actually I didn't meet him in person. I saw
him on film. As a writer on the ten o'clock news I would screen
much of the film sent in from the state capitol by McCuen each
day. Chick sent a lot of film too, rolls of it. He would delight
in sitting down with a state representative or senator for a
long talk about some obscure legislation. His stuff rarely made
the ten o'clock show but went on the earlier newscasts where
there was more time to fill. If our ten o'clock producer didn't
see the story on the news wires, it didn't go. But Chick was
making many friends in Springfield. They all thought they were
appearing on Chicago TV every day. Chick was a fixture in the
bar every night at the State House Inn across the street from the
capitol. He had a very healthy expense account.

In Chicago there's always a scandal around the next corner.
At the time Charles McCuen was running our Springfield news
coverage a famous Secretary of State named Paul Powell died
while in office. In Illinois the Secretary of State issues licenses
for every motor vehicle in the state and for every motor vehicle
operator. Powell was 68 years old when his body was found in a
hotel room in Rochester Minnesota in October of 1970. He was
being treated at the Mayo Clinic for heart disease. Paul Powell

was a Democrat who served for many years in the Illinois House and rose to be speaker of that body for four years before getting elected Secretary of State. A colorful and popular politician, top public officials of both parties mourned his passing.

A life long bachelor, Powell had resided in a suite at Springfield's St. Nicholas Hotel. Two months after his death a bombshell hit. Local officials disclosed that the executor of his will found hundreds of thousands of dollars in cash in shoe boxes and brief cases in closets in the hotel room. There were also cases of whiskey and other items, all presumably gifts to the Secretary which gave new meaning to Powell's often quoted statement following a Democratic election victory: "I can smell the meat a cookin." The estate also included over sixty thousand shares of stock in seven Illinois race tracks. Mr. Powell had been in government most of his life and never earned more than thirty thousand dollars a year.

Needless to say a media frenzy descended on Springfield Illinois in the coming weeks. NBC in Chicago assigned Charles McCuen to cover it full time. One of the first things Chick did was rent the old Powell suite at the St. Nick Hotel. He promptly threw a big cocktail party. Guests were thrilled as they kept finding five and ten dollar bills hidden behind curtains and under chair cushions. Chick's expense reports were legendary in the Chicago newsroom. The Powell story gradually faded from the headlines. Nothing much ever happened. When the estate was finally settled in 1978 it was worth 4.6 million dollars.

Chick was one of the best story tellers I ever met. When I first heard him tell the story about the New Years party in France with Sergeant Ackerman it was on a news broadcast in Chicago. I was moved and asked him about it. He said he occasionally repeated it over the years in different broadcast venues around holidays. He always asked for the Ackerman son to contact him. But that never happened.

In 1966 one of the worst mass murders in American history happened on the South side of Chicago. Eight young student nurses were found stabbed or strangled to death in their townhouse dormitory near a community hospital. At least one of the young women was raped. But one of the young nurses survived. She had hidden under a bed and would later bear witness to the awful crime. The murderer had also left fingerprints in the town house.

Within a few days police arrested a twenty-five year old longshoreman and drifter named Richard Speck. Speck was an ex convict with a long history of petty crime, drug and alcohol abuse. The story was front page news for many months.

Because of the publicity surrounding the case a Cook County Judge ordered a change of venue to Peoria, Illinois about 150 miles Southwest of Chicago. The trial was set to begin on April 3rd, 1967. An Army of media descended on Peoria. Presiding Judge Herbert Paschen set strict rules for press coverage of the trial and issued only twenty-five press credentials for access to the courtroom. NBC in Chicago sent Charles "Chick" McCuen. The Associated Press sent F. Richard Ciccone who would later become Managing Editor of the Chicago Tribune and an author. The veteran McCuen and young Ciccone hit it off right away. Both were pretty good imbibers and soon found a nifty lounge in town where they spent their evenings discussing trial testimony and other tall tales. But McCuen would have to sit out much of the trial due to a nationwide strike by the American Federation of Radio and Television Artists of which he was a member. During the walkout Chick was promptly hired as maitre "d at the restaurant where Ciccone and he and other reporters hung out. At the CBS network the famed anchorman Walter Cronkite honored the picket line and was replaced by a good looking young program manager named Arnold Zenker.

In Peoria the Speck trial was equally brief, less that

two weeks. The jury, which had heard testimony from an eyewitness and evidence of Speck's fingerprints at the murder scene, deliberated for less than an hour. Richard Speck was found guilty and sentenced to death. That sentence was later overturned and Richard Speck would die many years later in prison.

During my time at NBC I would come across more than one great story that Chick McCuen had done in the past. To mark the 20th anniversary of D-Day (the allied invasion of Europe in World War II) Chick went to the little town of Metropolis in Southern Illinois close to the Kentucky border. There he interviewed a man named John Steele, who had been with the 82nd Airborne Division on D-Day. Actually Steele parachuted behind enemy lines at midnight before the Normandy landing. He was thirty-three years old and still a private even though he had fought through Africa and Italy earlier in the war. The operation was costly for the 82nd. Many of the paratroopers missed their landing zones and landed instead in the little village of St. Mare Eglise. The town had been bombarded by our artillery and fires lit up the sky. The descending airmen were easy targets for the Germans. Unfortunately or fortunately, Private Steele landed on one of the spires of the town Church where he hung by his parachute.

Steele had a good view of the carnage below him. He was wounded by shrapnel and played dead when Germans came by. Eventually the Germans cut him down and took him prisoner. In the movie "The Longest Day" Steel's part is played by actor/comedian Red Buttons. Within a couple of days Steele managed to escape as Americans retook the town. On that anniversary of D-Day in 1964 Chick broadcast his interview with John Steele who had attained the rank of First Sergeant by the time he was discharged.

Twenty years later in 1984, Chick was long gone from NBC.

I had a segment on the early news called "The Notebook." My producer, Joe Howard, wanted me to include a piece on D-Day and he told of Chick's interview with John Steele so many years before. We were able to dig it out of the archives and put it on the air that night. I made some calls to Metropolis, IL to see if I could talk to John Steele. I learned that he had died of throat cancer in 1969. One of his relatives told me that John was older than many of the other boys who went to war. He had been out of work much of the depression and enlisted in the paratroopers because there was an extra fifteen dollars pay per month. Today an effigy of Steele and his parachute hang from that steeple in St. Mare Eglise and a tavern on the town square is named after him.

When he left NBC Chick McCuen went to work for the State of Illinois. We used to see him a lot when we went to cover the legislature. He was always very helpful. and still had great yarns to tell. I remember at some point he quit drinking and tried to get his old colleagues to go with him to church bingo games where he could spend evening hours in sobriety. Still later he got back into journalism and produced documentary films on state legislatures around the country.

Charles McCuen died in 1995 at the age of 74.

PAT BOYLE

Circa 1974

*A*s *a reporter I got to know many lawyers in Chicago. Most were flamboyant, a few were scholarly, all had a healthy portion of ego. By far the most memorable was one Charles A. "Pat" Boyle. He had been an assistant U.S. attorney and might have worked briefly in a couple of law firms but that never worked out. He was a lone cowboy. Outrageous, preposterous, zany were just a few words that aptly described him. He was also a compassionate man. He truly believed in helping the little guy who was being kicked around. A dapper dresser, he liked to quote the old saying:"you've got to dress British and think Yiddish." Central casting would have dubbed him the Irish priest. I think that's why he got so many great cases. People with troubles thought he was hearing their confession. He loved to sing and smile.*

The young man in the jail cell was Johnny Price who was accused of murder. He was with his attorney who had been appointed by the Cook County Circuit Court because young Price and his family couldn't afford their own. Johnny Price was a handsome young black man who looked like he could take on the world. But he had a big problem. He had a severe stutter and really couldn't speak. His attorney was Pat Boyle

who had trouble communicating with his client. At some point
Boyle discovered his client could sing clearly. Many years later
Boyle couldn't remember the name of the song or what made
him break into it in that Cook County jail cell with Johnny
Price. To Boyle's surprise the young man responded in song, in
beautiful clear tones. There was no stuttering. What followed
were musical interviews in which Boyle got Johnny Price's side
of the story.

The murder had taken place in a dingy second floor
apartment on South Washtenaw Street on the West side of
Chicago in February of 1970. The victim was 65 year old Mrs.
Clara Jenkins, an invalid confined to a wheel chair. She was
beaten senseless and died three days later in Cook County
Hospital. Before she died Mrs. Jenkins told her husband that
a young man named Lee Arthur Hodges was one of the young
men who had broken into the apartment. He was arrested
immediately. He implicated two other neighborhood men, his
cousin, Melvin Battle, and Johnny Price. By the time the case
got to court Hodges and Battle had made a deal with the state's
attorney's office. They could plead guilty to lesser charges in
return for their testimony against Johnny Price who they
claimed did the fatal beating. During the three day bench trial
they gave that testimony. Oddly enough both men told the
court they had sold two television sets stolen from the Jenkins
apartment, split the proceeds but gave Johnny Price nothing.

Price's father and sister both testified Johnny was home at
the time of the murder. Johnny Price had no previous criminal
record. He had a job in a nearby metal filing plant. He had
been in the U.S. Army but lasted only five months because
of his severe speech impediment. He was given an honorable
discharge. Boyle took a chance and put his client on the stand.
In what might have been a mini opera, Johnny denied the
crime. Still, Judge Dan Ryan found Price guilty of murder and

sentenced him to thirty years. Boyle never gave up on his client. There were more singing interviews and, after four years, the Appellate Court issued a complete reversal of the conviction. Johnny Price, who had become a top boxer in prison, was released after serving more than three years.

Sometimes justice is slow in Cook County.

PART III
Tiny Tales

Items that stuck in my mind

Live Television

1977

AT WABASH AND Lake Streets in Chicago the elevated tracks curve abruptly and make a ninety degree turn to go Westbound. There are four such turns in downtown Chicago as the train tracks form what is known as the "Loop".

People who regularly ride the Chicago Transit Authority will tell you of a recurring nightmare. The train is making that grinding turn around one of the curves and suddenly the cars roll off the tracks, tumbling to the crowded street below.

This did happen once and I was there . I didn't actually see the tumbling of the cars but I was there moments afterward with a camera crew.

Two cars were dangling from the elevated structure and another lay on the street. Fire trucks, ambulances and other emergency vehicles were scattered about the intersection. A priest, with stole around his neck and black book in hand ministered to a man on a stretcher as he waited to be taken away.

"Out of the way!," a burly fireman bellowed to onlookers as he tried to move a fire hose around them.

It was chaotic. Everything was happening fast and my

cameraman was shooting all of it as best he could. He couldn't move fast enough. There wasn't time to record it all.

Through all of the noise I could hear moaning of those who had been injured and were still being treated at the scene by paramedics.

Then I heard a panicky voice which startled me for a moment. It came from my two way radio. "We're going to live coverage. You have to set up for live coverage immediately."

"We can't go live yet. We're still shooting. They're still moving bodies out of here and there's a fire going. To set up live we'd have to go back to the truck on Wacker Drive. There's too much going on." The truck was the new mini cam van with the big microwave dish on top. It was February 4, 1977 and the mini-cam unit was a new breakthrough for television news. It could go anywhere and broadcast live at a moment's notice. In practice, though, the live shots were mostly breathless reporters talking in the dark rather than actual news footage.

"OK," said my assignment desk, "we'll send a courier in to get your video but we still want you to set up for a live shot ."

I was holding the two way to my ear and looking at some of the bystanders. They looked at me as though I had desecrated a holy place. A big fireman came growling by: "Keep that camera out of the way!"

More emergency vehicles were arriving at the scene. One of the el train cars was dangling precariously from the tracks.

The assignment desk kept screaming on the two way to get set up for a live shot. But I couldn't do it. We were already inside a police perimeter that had been set up. I told the desk I couldn't leave just yet and I knew the guy was furious. "Keep shooting!" I told my cameraman.

Eventually a courier found us and took our videotape. "You better set up for a live shot, Pete. They're really ticked off back there. They told me to bring you in if you didn't want to do it."

So I went and set up for the live report. We had to go to Wacker Drive, a couple of blocks away. I dutifully spoke into the camera. Behind you could see only flashing lights in the darkness.

Twelve people died and one hundred eighty were injured. Some of the victims were pedestrians crushed by the falling rail cars.

Sometime later I found out that I had come very close to being fired that night. I also learned that they had used our initial footage all night long during the program interruptions. Oh well. This was the start of the live television craze. I was reminded of an old cartoon in the New Yorker. A reporter with a camera behind him is talking to a man standing in front of a closed door. "You'll never believe what's going on in this room!" exclaims the man. "Tell me about it," replies the reporter.

St. Gabe's

Circa 1984

W HEN YOU WORKED nights at NBC in Chicago's Merchandise Mart you were allowed to park in the garage beneath the building after five o'clock in the afternoon. People could still park on the street in those days, over by the river with no parking meters, but nobody wanted to leave their car there at night. There were some nasty dogs that hung out by the river. Some writer was chased by one of these animals after the ten o'clock news. This was before the East Bank Club and other developments that make up today's trendy River North District. So night workers would get out there after 5PM and pull their cars into the building.

There was this nice little older gentleman, a uniformed guard, at the garage to admit you. He was as Irish as they come in Chicago. Once he approached me and asked if I could do a story on his parish, St. Gabriel's, which was celebrating its 100th anniversary.

So I pitched the story and was sent out to St. Gabe's where a young assistant pastor took me around and told me the story.

The neighborhood was called Canaryville, home to Irish immigrants who came to work in the nearby Union Stockyards. Apparently wild pigs had roamed that area, feeding on garbage.

Locals called them Canaries and thus the neighborhood got its name. The yards were a fearful place, as chronicled in Upton Sinclair's classic muckraking book, The Jungle. The stink from the slaughter houses was quite noticeable a hundred years later and even for some time after the Yards closed in the 1970's. In the late nineteenth century the Irish workers needed plenty of help especially on the spiritual side.

They would soon find a champion in the Catholic priest who came to serve them. His name was Father Maurice J. Dorney, a native of Massachusetts who was raised in Chicago where he later was ordained a priest.

When he came to Canaryville in 1880 he stayed at the fashionable Transit House Hotel at the Stockyards. It was a forerunner to the famous Stockyard Inn which came after the turn of the century. Dorney was a very personable fellow, well educated and a great conversationalist. At evening dinners he soon made friends with famous names in the meat business such as Armour, Morris and Swift. With their help the priest made arrangements to have Sunday Mass at the hotel which he said in a rented room while the parish waited for a new home.

Father Dorney engaged the famous architect and urban planner, Daniel Burnham to draw up the plans for the new St. Gabriel's, a structure of Gothic Revival design which still stands today at the corner of 45th St. and Wallace Avenue.

Daniel Burnham would later gain fame as the manager of the 1893 World's Columbian Exposition and creator of the famed "White City" on Chicago's South side. He and his partner, John Wellborn Root, designed the first so-called skyscraper in Chicago and the Flatiron building in New York along with many other landmarks.

As pastor of St. Gabriel's, Maurice Dorney became quite the newsmaker. At age fifty he received a law degree. He mediated many of the labor disputes that erupted in the Stockyards. The working men and the managers of the packing houses respected his judgement. The newspapers gave him the title "King of the Yards." (All of this being told to me with great relish by a young assistant pastor one hundred years later.)

Dorney also was deeply involved in the independence movement in Ireland. He was a member of Clan Na Gael, or United Brotherhood of Americans in support of Irish independence, and was a delegate to their national convention. He once went to Ireland to help the Irish leader Charles Parnell. He also testified at a Chicago murder trial in behalf of the defendant who was accused of murdering a critic of the Clan Na Gael movement.

In 1889 the Chicago Tribune published an article asking the Archbishop of Chicago to transfer Father Dorney to some country parish where he couldn't cause so much trouble.

But the young priest was most amused when he told this about Father Dorney. The Pastor was fond of going to Florida during Chicago's cold winter months. A strong supporter of temperance, Father Dorney led a movement to keep taverns out of the neighborhoods and restrict them to main thoroughfares. On one occasion, before leaving for Florida, he instructed from the pulpit that it was OK to open a tavern on Forty-Seventh or Halsted Streets but definitely not on side streets near family residences.

Upon returning this particular year he found that a couple of parishioners had disobeyed his order. When these people showed up at mass he made them stand up so he could reprimand them with very caustic remarks.

When he died at age sixty-three, Father Dorney was given a huge Chicago send off. More than a thousand people attended including public officials and members of the famous meat packing families, the Armour's the Swifts and the Morris's.

Every available funeral limo in Chicago took part in the procession.

The funeral arrangements were handled no doubt by Thomas McInerney and Sons on South Wallace Ave. It's still in business today as it has been since 1873. For at least a hundred years it has used in its advertising a poem by T. J. O'Donnell.

Bring out the lace curtains and call McInerney;
I'm nearing the end of my life's pleasant journey.
Send quick for the priest, just tell him I'm dying
my last minutes on earth so swiftly are flying.
Tell dear Father Dorney I'm meeting my maker
(He's losing his old collection up taker.)
Then pull down the shades and light up the candles
Call the O'Briens, the Caseys and Randalls.
The Murphy;s, the Burkes, the Bradys and all.
Tell them your darlin has answered God's call.
Call Schultz the fat butcher and order some meat;
Let watchers who sit through the night have a treat.
There's good Mrs. Smith who is sure to bring cake.
Please ask her advice in conducting my wake.
Bring out the lace curtains and call McInerney;
I'm nearing the end of my life's pleasant journey.

FORGIVENESS

June 1977

Nick Comito was shot down in his backyard in a modest, racially changing neighborhood on Chicago's West side. One of the bullets entered his head and, as the doctors said, it literally exploded his eyes, blinding him for life.

This brutal act drew widespread media attention but there was something else which rarely happens after such crimes. In the hospital, right after the shooting, Comito said he felt no anger, no hate for the young man who shot him.

A year after the incident I interviewed Mr. Comito in his garden on a beautiful Spring day. Nick was learning to walk with a cane and to read with Braille. The garden, which he so loved, was a reality only through smell and hearing and touch. He told me he prayed every day for his assailant.

Nick and his wife decided to stay in the neighborhood after the shooting. Indeed, it was difficult for me to visualize the act of violence that took place in the beautiful little garden- yard a year before.

The young man who shot Nick was sentenced to one hundred to two hundred years in prison. His name didn't seem important at the time. What I remember most was that gentle, humane man who offered a small flash of hope to a world of anger and violence.

SNOW NEWS

Timeless

I KNOW SOMETHING ABOUT snow. I grew up in Buffalo, New York and I spent my career as a television newsman in Chicago. So I believe I can speak with some authority on snow.

I know, for example, that snow comes every year to many regions of the United States: the Great Lakes, the Northeast, the Midwest, the plains and mountains and other places. It happens during the winter months.

Yet local TV news programs regard snow and winter as something no one has seen before.

I'm not talking about a blizzard that paralyzes New York City, or a storm so great that voters defeat the legendary Chicago Democratic machine, or when thousands of homes lose power for extended periods of time. Those are real news stories.

I'm talking about this: GOOD EVENING LADIES AND GENTLEMEN I'M HARRY ANCHORMAN. TWO AND A HALF INCHES OF SNOW FELL ON CHICAGO TODAY AND WE'RE ALL OVER THE STORY. AND I'M DENISE BLONDESHELL. RIGHT YOU ARE HARRY. OUR LIVE, TEAM COVERAGE BEGINS RIGHT NOW!

LET'S GO TO JIM TRENCHCOAT WHO'S LII----VE OVER THE KENNEDY EXPRESSWAY. Trenchcoat: WELL,

AS YOU CAN SEE, DENISE AND HARRY TRAFFIC HAS
SLOWED TO A CRAWL. (Actually the traffic doesn't seem
to be all that bad.) POLICE AND OTHER OFFICIALS ARE
ASKING MOTORISTS TO TAKE IT EASY. IT'S VERY, VERY
SLIPPERY OUT HERE. AND I'M HAPPY TO REPORT THAT
THE CITY HAS PUT EVERY AVAILABLE SALT TRUCK
ON THE STREET. HERE'S A TIP. IF YOU GO OUT, MAKE
SURE YOU HAVE GLOVES AND A SCRAPER IN THE CAR.
AND THAT SPRAY DE-ICING STUFF ISN'T A BAD IDEA
EITHER. BACK TO YOU DENISE AND HARRY.

Harry and Denise then do a quick flip to the weatherman.
But he's only predicting scattered flurries for the rest of the
night and not much tomorrow. So the anchors grab it right
back from him. Now they throw it to Mary Breathless who's live
out in suburban Barrington. Mary is wearing a pretty fur hat (a
fashionable hat is now a must for female reporters in winter)
and has picked up a handful of snow, letting it drop slowly
through her gloved hand to the ground. And Mary tells us that
it has snowed in the suburbs too, and, can you believe this, the
children are having a ball with it. (pictures of children sledding
and throwing snowballs.) WELL AT LEAST SOMEBODY IS
ENJOYING THIS WEATHER, DENISE AND HARRY!

And so the newscast plods on. Commercial breaks occur.
And the snow story continues. A reporter is standing in front
of a stockpile of blue salt telling the audience not to worry.
There's plenty of salt. Another reporter is live at the city's
snow command babbling on and on. And there has to be an
appearance by the city's snow command chief. Chicago is still
using a tough-looking guy named Sanchez. But I predict the PR
people will soon prevail and Sanchez will be replaced on the air
by a gorgeous male or female that rivals the TV people.

Why do they do it? I think they do it because it's easy. It takes
hard work to develop a really interesting story. With snow, you

just send out the trucks and the reporters. Not much thinking is involved. The anchors and the reporters all get a lot of face time on camera. They like that. The producers fill their news block. The management sees a sense of urgency that their high priced consultants have told them must come across on the air to hold the viewers. The audience is drowsy. Everybody is happy.

The late Mike Royko wrote about television's coverage of winter in his Tribune column several years ago. "I turn on the TV News and there's a guy with a microphone standing out in a shopping center and he's saying that, even though it's cold, people are still going out to do their shopping, like this is some big surprise. And he says we should dress warm if we go out. How come the local TV stations talk to us like we're all a bunch of helpless morons?"

Making a simple winter snowfall into a major news story is an exercise that's been going on too long in local TV news. I recall being sent on such a light snow story more than twenty years ago. It was a live shot out on some expressway and my cameraman made a very perceptive comment. "Why are we doing this?" he said. "We're going to tell people it's snowing outside, when they can look out the window and see it for themselves. It's so stupid."

THE PRESIDENT IN TOWN

Circa 1974

THERE WAS THIS time in March of 1974 when President Richard M. Nixon came to Chicago and I was sent to cover it. I should explain how television covered an event like this at the time. It was like a small army being mobilized. Extra camera crews and couriers were hired. Credentials were issued to everyone taking part in the coverage, so that police and Secret Service agents could recognize you as a media person The Secret Service wanted everyone's Social Security number. Elaborate plans were made to place reporters and camera crews at various locations where the President was supposed to be, like at the airport on his arrival, at his hotel or in a ballroom where he is scheduled to make a speech. If there are demonstrators along the way then a crew must be assigned to cover them. There were always demonstrators against the Viet Nam war. Plans were made to pick up the thousands of feet of film exposed and get it back to the house for processing. On these occasions I don't think anyone really knew what we would do with all this footage. The idea was to get it all together and then decide later how the story would go.

Many times a presidential visit would result in only two minutes of air time on the news that night. Still, a President's visit to Chicago was an event to be covered massively. I don't remember anyone talking about it openly, I think everyone knew the real reason for this enormous effort and expenditure. This was a time of assassinations, riots, war and all sorts of insane happenings. And television, which brought so many events into the American living room would somehow be remiss if another one was not duly recorded. No one really thought it would happen but there was always that possibility. Some of the crews called it the death watch.

Then too there was also the possibility of a lesser happening such as the President falling down or someone shouting something nasty at him. An example comes to mind which will give you an idea of how little manpower was spared to make sure the coverage went off OK. In 1968 President Lyndon Johnson came to Chicago the day after he announced he would not run for re-election. I was a brand new writer in the NBC newsroom on the nineteenth floor of the Merchandise Mart. I was very impressed by the beehive of activity around me. Since I had no assignment at the moment I asked someone if I could help. A network deskman handed me a telephone and told me to hold on to it. I didn't have to talk to anyone, it was a line to the Conrad Hilton Hotel where the President was scheduled to speak. We needed to keep it open at all costs because it could be a vital link to NBC News operations in the field.

I took a vacant slot at the desk and pressed the phone to my ear, feeling very important and part of the bustle of activity around me. The time passed slowly and I kept hoping something would happen. Finally, after about an hour, I blurted a big hello into the phone. And, surprise, there was another hello from the other end. It turned out he was a courier at a pay phone at the Hilton. He said he was holding the phone for some producer for the Today Show.. We made small talk for a few minutes and I must have held that phone for another hour before someone came along and gave me something more important to do. I don't know if the line was ever used but it was available. There were no cell phones or social media in those days.

More often than not, my assignments on these occasions did not require any great reportorial skills. For example, I might be sent to the Military section of O'Hare Airport to cover the arrival of Air Force One. We would film the President getting off, waving, getting in his car and driving off. Then we would ship the film and I had to radio the desk that the President had landed and was on his way downtown. That was all we had to do, no big deal.

On that particular day in the Spring of 1974. I was assigned outside the Conrad Hilton Hotel. President Nixon was making a speech inside. Things were going real bad for the President then. Watergate was overwhelming him and the scandal would soon force him out of office. Our job along with the other crews on the street was to film the President leaving the hotel.

I must say that, despite the minor role I played in these lofty affairs, I got a big kick out of it. I liked having two way radios blaring away inside and outside the hotel. reporting the slightest bit of information to the desk, like the size of the crowd at the front door. Teddy Elbert, an NBC Network News producer was out there that day with a crew. He had as much irreverence for what we were doing as I did. So we had a lot of fun.

I used to enjoy observing the Secret Service agents. They all looked alike, conservative business suits, modified haircuts, an ear piece for their small radios and a special lapel button that identified them to each other and anyone else who might be interested. They were all easily identified and I wondered about this. Weren't they supposed to blend in with the crowd? Wouldn't it be to their advantage if nobody knew who they were? I hope they had some people working under cover. The way it was the most unsophisticated observer could pick them out easily.

Anyway it was fun to watch them, giving everybody the evil eye. Another thing bothered me. I seldom saw any of these men (there were very few women agents in those days) looking up at the surrounding buildings. I rather expected this and watched for it but rarely saw any of them look up. Perhaps there were others who checked these points of view. It was cold that day and it drizzled on and off.

A crowd of about 200 demonstrators had gathered across Michigan Avenue. A police line kept them on that side of the street. They appeared to be a good natured group, certainly not as menacing as demonstrators I had seen in the past. One kid held a sign that read: Nobody likes a crooked Dick. They were in a good mood. Occasionally a long haired cab driver would go by raising a clenched fist out the window and the crowd would roar its approval. Everything seemed to be under control.

Then an overly ambitious police sergeant marched a platoon of cops into the demonstrators., dividing them in half. If anything might have caused this group to be troublesome this would have been it. But nothing much happened. One young man gave the cops a hard time and he was arrested. A veteran newspaper reporter, watching all this, recalled the 1968 convention riots in Chicago. "The police really haven't learned much, have they," he remarked, shaking his head.

Nothing of any real significance happened that day. But there is one little flash that comes back to me now and then. I'm not sure why. It has to do with the way Nixon left the hotel. Mind you, my task was just to film the President going into the hotel and out. In those days the White House people were a bit paranoid and intent on keeping reporters and photographers away from the President. It didn't take long for me to figure out they were going to bring him out the side door. I got the crew over there and waited. There weren't many people around. Police had blocked off the street. A few still photographers, my crew and myself were kept on the opposite side of the street. Soon the Presidential limousine pulled around. The staff cars and the Secret Service cars lined up. Some fire exit doors to the hotel opened. Out came President Richard M. Nixon. He got into the limo and sped off. He had eluded the bulk of the media and the demonstrators.

But we got him. We did our job and duly recorded the President's coming and going. None of these pictures ever hit the air. Years later some NBC official told me all these cans of film were gathering dust in some warehouse in New Jersey.

But time was running out for President Nixon. Watergate kept building in the coming months and the President and his people were hounded by the media. In August Richard Nixon resigned his presidency.

During all the Watergate hullabaloo a funny thing happened at home. On several occasions as I was going to or from work I noticed my three sons lying on the floor watching television. They were usually doing that. Only this time they were watching Watergate hearings. It was all Watergate. There was nothing else on. This was before the cable explosion. The boys seemed to be paying attention. TV generally has that effect. I remember as a kid in the early days of TV we'd watch the test pattern when that was the only thing on.

So I asked the little guys what they thought of President Nixon and Watergate. There was silence. Finally, my oldest boy Patrick, who was all of seven years old said: "I kind of feel sorry for Nixon. Everybody's after him." Few such words of compassion for President Nixon were spoken at the time.

BACK PAY

S HE WAS ASKING about a story I knew nothing about. I could have looked at the script of our latest newscast and just said I was sorry we did not have such a report. Why did I get this call anyway? Maybe I was the only reporter in the newsroom. Maybe the phone person thought I might know something cause I covered City Hall. I would field hundreds of such calls. Usually the caller had the facts wrong or had heard some bogus report on the street. Sorry. Thanks for calling. Once in awhile there was a real news tip involved.

I remember her name was Mrs. Wallace. And there was something in her voice that made me want to hear more. Was it anguish or just love that I heard in the tone of her voice. She was talking about her husband.

He was a retired Chicago policeman who had served more than thirty years. He had suffered a stroke some time back and was confined to a wheel chair.

"You see Mr. Nolan, he can't talk, but he's very aware of everything and he has a great appetite. I'd love to cook him a steak once in awhile. But my funds are limited. We had to move to a small apartment. I thought I heard on the news that the city might pay policemen who worked during the depression."

I told her I wasn't aware of the story and asked her to explain. This is what she said: During the Depression the city of Chicago was broke, unable to pay its employees. Many were laid off. The city needed police and fire protection. Many of these men stayed on the job. They felt a sense of duty. The city agreed to pay them script money which could be redeemed when revenue was available.

Well, the Great Depression ended and the Police and Firemen went back to work and everybody was happy. Somehow the city never got around to redeeming the script pay.

Efforts were made over the years. Mrs. Wallace said that Alderman Ed Burke, a former police officer, had tried. But the lawyers got involved. Too much time had passed. Many had died. The accounting would be a nightmare.

I'm sure the Wallaces are long gone now as well as all those other duty-bound Police and firemen who stayed on the job without pay, protecting the citizens of Chicago.

I can still remember the woman's voice on the phone. It was full of hope and love. Yet I think she knew it was a lost cause. "That money would sure come in handy right now," she said. I'd love to give my husband a nice steak dinner."

THAT NICE LITTLE LADY AT THE LOAN COMPANY

Circa 1974

MARSHALL, ILLINOIS WAS a little Farm Community South of Chicago. The town was about twenty miles West of Terre Haute, Indiana. The only time I ever went there was to report on a scandal. Six months earlier it was discovered that the little Marshall Loan Company was hopelessly insolvent. The owner, Sylvia Ritter Millhouse, had died a few months earlier. She had been loved and trusted by everyone. After months of scrutinizing her antiquated book keeping system, the accountants found liabilities of one million seven hundred thousand dollars. The assets at best came to about two hundred thousand dollars. No one was sure where all the money went. Mrs. Hilda Rhoads, a widow, lost fifty three thousand dollars. Another town resident, Ira Cooper, issued a limited series of gold commemorative medals and wood nickels with the inscription: Marshall, Illinois the town taken to the cleaners by a nice little old lady. Orders came in from all over the country. Everybody in town seemed to like Mrs. Millhouse. She lived in a modest little house near the outskirts. Some old timers remember expensive parties she threw. They said she squandered money on her son, that she built him a house with a pool next door. Was she a swindler or just a nice old lady who couldn't keep books? And what happened to all the money?

HOW GERALDO
SCOOPED ME

Circa 1982

I WAS SENT TO do a story on the old Lexington Hotel on South Michigan Avenue. It was famous because the gangster, Al Capone had once had his headquarters there. It had been an elegant place in its heyday but by the 80's it had become abandoned and fallen victim to vandals and winos. Just before World War II, under the name of the New Michigan Hotel it was one of the city's most notorious bordellos. Capone took up residence in the 1920's and it became his headquarters for bootlegging and gambling. His gang took up most of two floors. Capone's own suite boasted a private kitchen with two full time chefs. The bath was decorated in lavender tile and matching fixtures. A policeman at the time described the quarters as fit for French royalty. In the basement there were escape tunnels leading to the Metropole Hotel across the street. When police raided the Lexington they sometimes found it deserted. I had been in the hotel once before, probably for some Capone anniversary. I remember a worker telling me about Capone's safe still being in the basement, He said it was open but there was nothing in it but some broken bottles. He asked if I wanted to go down and see it. I deferred when he warned of many rats in the basement. On this assignment in the early

1980's, the Sun Bow Foundation, a not for profit group, had just purchased the property. Sun Bow helped poor, inner city women get experience in the construction trades. They had begun renovation of the building. The hotel that once housed a notorious gangster and later a brothel was soon going to have an international museum devoted to the accomplishments of women.

Several years later I was amused to see that Geraldo Rivera, the young television news star, was going to do a program on the Lexington Hotel. This two hour special was called the Mystery of Al Capone's vault. They were going to open this vault on live television. The hype was really great. The IRS was going to be there in case any cash was found that could be declared as back taxes owed by Capone. A mob of reporters and camera crews showed up. Unfortunately Geraldo and his Hollywood producers relied heavily on the research of a man named Harold Rubin who claimed to be a Capone expert. Many Chicagoans remembered him from years before as "Weird" Harold Rubin, the proprietor of a string of pornography stores in the South loop. Weird Harold was constantly in trouble with the cops and appeared frequently in the newspapers and on TV. The Geraldo show aired on Apr. 26, 1986. Somehow a sealed vault had been discovered in the basement of the Lexington Hotel. It took a lot of construction work to get to the vault and then some sophisticated tools to open it. The final climactic scene: Geraldo with a few broken bottles and dirt. He sang the song Chicago.

It wasn't all a bust. The Mystery of Al Capone's vault, syndicated by Tribune Broadcasting, had a national audience of thirty million people, the most watched special that year. Many years later Geraldo Rivera told an interviewer he got Tequila drunk after that show. I took a little ribbing at the office from people who remembered my story of the Lexington. "How come you never found that vault? Geraldo scooped you."

PART IV
THE COMMENTATOR

From 1978 to 1981 I did commentaries on the ten o'clock news at WMAQ-TV Channel 5. As I look at these writings nearly forty years later I make this observation. The things that we find amusing or make us sad, the things that annoy us, don't change much with the passing of the decades. Here are some of the issues that caught my attention so long ago.

THEY BURIED
JIMMY NOLAN

7-13-79

THEY BURIED A guy named Jimmy Nolan today. He was only thirty-three years old. Jimmy was a cop, "a homocide dick" to use the jargon of the street. His death was not front page news, a small item in the obituary section. Still it was untimely. He was recovering from surgery. Suddenly blood clots developed and he was gone. One of those statistics in modern day medicine that aren't supposed to happen but on rare occasion do.

I was not a close friend of Jimmy Nolan's, (and, by the way, he was no relation to me), But I did cover a shootout that he investigated one time. I ran into him on the street several times after that and we had conversations about police work. In my years as a newsman I've come into contact with all kinds of police officers all over the country. Chicago cops are a special breed. There are few that you feel lukewarm about. You either love them or hate them.

Jimmy Nolan was the lovable kind. I'm sure that after twelve years as a policeman he acquired the normal amount of cynicism that goes along with the job of cleaning up after society's mistakes. But the hardening of the heart that sometimes afflicts veteran officers never set in with Jimmy. He was a compassionate cop with that rare understanding of the basic frailty of the human beings he dealt with. As I said, his passing is not page one news but I think the citizens of Chicago should be aware of this loss.

NEW MAYOR TAKES BODYGUARDS FROM THE OLD MAYOR

If you think politics is nasty today. Take a look at this story in Chicago at the end of the 70's.

July 18, 1979

I visited a fiend of mine who moved to Chicago recently and was writing a letter home. "They're never going to believe it," he said. "Believe what?" I asked. He proceeded to tell me that he was giving the folks back home all the news that had happened in Chicago recently.

He opened with the story of the new Mayor taking the police bodyguards away from the old Mayor. Something about the bodyguards being annoyed because they had to change the diapers of the old Mayor's infant son. Then the old Mayor's wife, a prominent socialite, confronts the new Mayor at a block party and asks her if she can sleep at night.

He went on to tell them about the night he went to a White Sox double header. A disc jockey goes out in center field and blows up some disco records. Thousands of rock, not Sox fans pour onto the field and the Sox have to forfeit the second game.

Then my friend wrote about the circuit court judge who is being investigated for making wild and irrational speeches in his courtroom and for falling asleep and snoring during a trial he was hearing. It seems this particular judge was being considered for the federal bench.

"Wait a minute! Don't write anymore," I told my friend, "That's plenty for them to swallow in one letter." Then I advised him to close with one of the standard disclaimers. This never would have happened if Mayor Daley were alive. Or, this could only happen in Chicago.

DRIVING THE KIDS TO FLORIDA

Ah, the family vacation was and still is a good yarn on a slow news day.

8-19-05

Around 1975 my wife and I and our six children began driving to the panhandle of Florida for Spring break vacations.

The first year we went in an old Chevy station wagon the kids called the yellow vomit. After an overnight delay because of a busted fuel pump in Kentucky, we eventually made it to Florida.

The next year I wised up and bought a van. I quickly found out that the high jinks six kids can perform on a long road trip are not diminished because you have a little more room.

Mary's touching me with her bare foot! Patrick hit me! Matt has to go to the bathroom! How long before we get out of Indiana? Are we still in Alabama? That's the way it went. I liked to tell friends the fighting began around Touhy Avenue, Chicago and it was downhill all the way to the Gulf of Mexico. My wife seemed oblivious to the chaos in the back as she gazed at the passing countryside. I'd hold the wheel with my left hand and try to grab one of the little culprits with my right, but they were too fast for me. I'd threaten to skip the next McDonald's stop, but that never worked cause dad got hungry too.

The trip took a day and a half. We'd overnight somewhere around Montgomery, Alabama. The next day, when that blue-green gulf appeared on the horizon, well, after a long Chicago winter, that was the payoff. That part of Florida wasn't as developed as it is today and there were long, untouched stretches of white sand beach. And what did my boys want to do as soon as we got there? They wanted a dollar to go play video games at Ski Ball City across the street.

In recent years my daughter Christine and my son Patrick started going back there with their families. They go in August right before school starts. This year they were joined by their younger brother Stephen and his family. They go to the same resort, Silver Dunes. The same beach guy, George, is still there to rent them their cabanas.

I know the kids have movies in the van when they're driving down these days. But the back seat battles haven't changed much over the years. I like to ask the grand kids: "Say, when did the fighting start on the way down to Florida?" The dutiful reply is: "It started at Touhy Ave., Papa." I love it.

AN ECONOMIC STORY

The state of the nations's economy doesn't change much over the years, just the economists.

7-26-79

Sometimes it's difficult to understand the complicated news about the state of our nation's economy. Every night men in pin striped suits appear on our television screens from Washington talking about OPEC oil prices, the price of gold, dollar devaluation. We hear goofy sounding words about the economy like deceleration and stagnation.

But there's a story out of San Antonio today that speaks to the problem more eloquently than a thousand Washington bureaucrats. A woman named Mattie Schultz was held in jail for twenty four hours after shoplifting about fifteen dollars worth of food at a supermarket. Mattie Schultz is 91 years old, the widow of a World War I veteran. She said she took the food because she was starving. She did have 48 dollars in her purse but she said that money was needed to pay rent and utility bills.

A United States Senator warned today about the possibility of another great depression. I hope he's wrong. Perhaps a widow stealing food to stay alive is one of those oddities that pop up in the news now and then. But there was something about this desperate woman's story that cried out for attention. "I wish I could close my eyes," Mrs. Schultz said, "I'm so tired of living." I hope the people in Washington heard that lament.

HEALTH SCARE
ON SCOTCH

The health scare story has been a staple of the news business for many years. Is that glass of red wine good or bad for you? Here's one from my day.

8-8-79

I have to admit I was a little concerned when I heard that story last night that some brands of Scotch whiskey contained a cancer causing agent. Having some familiarity with the product I decided to investigate. I called the Distilled Sprits Council of the United States which is headquartered in Washington, D.C. A gentleman there immediately knocked down the story. But, after all, whiskey is their business. You wouldn't expect them to bad rap their business. I decided the best way to check this would be to contact a heavy Scotch user. I immediately thought of an old friend in Buffalo, New York named Stick O'Day. You're probably wondering how someone would acquire a name like Stick. Well, Stick O'Day used to hang around the same tavern every night until the joint closed. Gradually, as the night wore on, people would leave the bar to go home. "Aren't you gonna stick around, aren't you gonna stick to closing," he would call out to no avail. Thus the name "Stick" stuck. Anyway Stick has been putting away the Scotch for years and when I reached him today at one of his favorite haunts he just laughed and laughed at this story about Scotch causing cancer. "You see kid," he said, "they've got it all wrong. It's the lemon peels and the soda and maybe the ice that's no good and causes all the problems, not the Scotch. The whiskey may turn your liver into hamburger but it won't give you cancer."

NASTY POLITICS

In 1979The Mayor of Chicago was Jane Byrne, the first woman to hold that office. She had defeated the incumbent Mayor who was part of the legendary Democratic machine. To say the least the woman was colorful and spunky. She endorsed Senator Ted Kennedy for President in his bid to oust the incumbent President, Jimmy Carter. The swing to Kennedy came a couple of weeks after she pledged her support to Carter.

The Mayor also backed an alderman named Ed Burke in a primary against the incumbent State's Attorney, Richard M. Daley, son the the late Mayor.

If you think politics is bitter and nasty today, especially with the appearance of President Donald Trump, I give you a commentary broadcast during the Illinois primary season of 1980. It was pretty rough and tumble then, but a little more fun.

3-11-80

We're in the last week of the campaign. There are bullet holes in Eddie Burke's campaign headquarters. Yesterday at the Democratic precinct captains' meeting, the voice of the late Mayor Richard J. Daley was heard from the balcony. The captains were momentarily shocked but it was only a tape recording, a prank. So were the Rich Daley balloons that sailed through the air. It brought to mind some wonderful events of elections past when Eddie Hanrahan fortune cookies were placed on the captains' tables or when John Hoellen brought a snake into city hall so he could drive it out. Last night a distraught Bridgeport woman called to say that Mayor Byrne is sending the building inspectors down on a Catholic Church where Rich Daley is supposed to speak.

Campaign signs are being torn down and put back up again. Wonderful lies are being told about the candidates. Threats are being made. Ted Kennedy may have to swallow the tab for a couple of Mayor Byrne's afternoon teas. When you stop to think about it, campaigning in Chicago hasn't changed much since the turn of the century when Hinky Dink Kenna and Bathouse John Coughlin ruled the first ward. And in the words of a great song back then: "..there were biters and fighters and Irish dynamiters."Oh what a lot of fun it is to be in the final days of a primary campaign.

TED KENNEDY AND ROGER MUDD

Before this same primary season beganTed Kennedy was contemplating a run for President like his brothers Bobby and Jack before him. But his heart didn't seem to be in it as indicated by this commentary.

11-5-79

Last night there was a program on CBS called Teddy which examined Senator Edward Kennedy of Massachusetts, his personality and his candidacy for President of the United States. According to the overnight rating services the program attracted only a minor share of the audience in the Chicago area. Kennedy should be happy about that because I think the program devastated him. Under tough questioning about Chappaquiddick Kennedy appeared confused, almost to the point of double talk. He even appeared bewildered when asked basic questions like why he wanted to be President or how he was different from President Carter. I must admit I was surprised by his performance as I was surprised last week when a Chicago ward committeeman told me he had discovered some serious opposition to Kennedy in his ward especially from women who he said were angry about Chappaquiddick and the Senator's widely publicized marital problems. Today, Alderman Roman Pucinski of the Northwest side 41st Ward, said a poll taken over the weekend showed Kennedy leading President Carter by only two percentage points. Nevertheless the Cook County Democratic Central Committee went ahead and endorsed Kennedy today. I asked several ward committeemen if they had seen the program last night. All of them said thy were watching "Jaws" on another channel. That's too bad. They should have seen the Kennedy show before they voted. But it's too late now.

ROLAND BURRIS

During my career racial issues were always in the news as they sadly seem to pop up today. Here's one of the nice stories of an African American getting elected to an obscure state wide office in Illinois. Corneal Davis, whose name is mentioned in this piece, is the subject of another story in this book called "Jim Crowe at the Abraham Lincoln Hotel."

1-8-79

Roland Burris is the first black man to be elected to a top state office in Illinois. You might remember that during the campaign his opponent ran a picture of Burris in HIS campaign commercials. We all knew what that was about. Although it was denied, the obvious intent was to let voters know that Roland Burris is a black man. What did the voters do? They elected Roland Burris Controller of Illinois. More than a million and a half citizens voted for this black man. So his inauguration today was indeed a milestone in Illinois History. Burris told us in his speech that before the ceremonies this morning he paid a visit to the tomb of Abraham Lincoln here in Springfield. And, as he stood alone, he wondered if Lincoln could see him, if he knew what was taking place today. It got me thinking about the History of Civil Rights in this country. More than a century has passed since President Lincoln moved to abolish slavery. Just over thirty years ago a man who is ending his career in the legislature, State Representative Corneal Davis was refused a room at the Abraham Lincoln Hotel down the street because he was black. Well, the Abraham Lincoln Hotel is torn down now. Corneal Davis is leaving and Roland Burris is just beginning. I don't know what kind of Controller Burris will be but I think everyone in Illinois can be proud he was elected. Burris said he came to the conclusion that somehow Lincoln knew what was going on here today. I liked that.

WASTEFUL BUREAUCRACY

IN 1980 Jimmy Carter , a Democrat, was the incumbent President of the United States and he was being challenged by Republican Ronald Reagan, a former actor and Governor of California. There was a third candidate, John Anderson, a moderate Republican from Illinois who ran as an independent.. Here is a campaign commentary that rings of government bureaucracy we still encounter today. The old government waste story.

10 13-80

A story in today's edition of the Chicago Sun Times caught my attention and I wish the three candidates for President could have read it. I think it represents what most voters in this country are fed up with. The story tells of a government created agency known as the Chicago Urban Transportation District. The Chicago Transportation District was created years ago to oversee transportation projects in the loop. But for many months now this agency has had nothing to do. And yet it has an annual budget of 1.2 million dollars, over 12 million dollars in the bank, expensive offices downtown, and a board whose five members are paid an annual salary of ten thousand dollars. They've met only twice this year. Most of the District's money comes from federal grants and local tax levies. You know what federal grants are? Those are things that don't cost us a cent because the money comes from the federal government. Will this Chicago Urban Transportation District cease and desist, now that it has nothing to do? Of course not. It will continue to ramble on. President Carter has told us not to look for simple solutions to economic problems. Maybe this economic problem is too simple or too small. But Carter or Reagan or Anderson might do well to pick up on some of these little items. It's this type of thing that has voters grinding their teeth every day.

THE EIGHTEEN WHEELER
BEHIND YOU

October 23, 1978

You're on an interstate highway in the passing lane. Suddenly you glance in the rear view mirror and there it is. A huge tractor trailer truck, his nose about to kiss your back end. The presence is menacing, almost saying to you: Get out of my way Bub or I'll run ya over!" Whoever said these guys are pros must be the same person who told us that lie that truckers know the best places on the road to eat. Illinois law says a driver must maintain a reasonable and prudent distance between him or her and the car ahead. Following too close is against the law. I note with chagrin that arrests for such violations by the State Police have been going down lately. I think they should be going up. I'm happy to report that at least one Judge in Illinois has ruled that a big truck tailgating a car could constitute an assault. I don't know what's causing these guys to drive like animals. Maybe it's all that lousy food they eat in the truck stops. I know I'll take some heat from all of the good truck drivers out there. I'm not talking about you. But some of your "good buddies", they ain't so good anymore.

NONE OF THE ABOVE

This commentary in the early nineties was about a movement that needed a revival in the Presidential election season of 2016.

March 16, 1992

Not long ago I mentioned the "None of the Above" movement. Some people out there have been pushing for a new line on our election ballots. None of the Above. You go into the voting booth an you look at candidates for a certain office, and say you don't like any of them. Then you would have the option of voting for None of the Above. And if None of the Above wins, then there would have to be a new election with new candidates. Politicians don't like this idea because it would be a nasty blow to their egos. I thought about this as I read recent polls which show that President Bush (George H.W.) would run roughly even against either Paul Tsongas or Bill Clinton. But here's the kicker. The polls say if you match Bush with an unnamed Democrat, he loses big, about 56 to 36 percent. So, when you see some of these mopes drooling through your TV sets saying how great they're doing in the primaries, just remember the real winner, None of the Above.

BACK TO SCHOOL

Then there's the perennial back to school story at summer's end. I wonder if this commentary still has legs today.

Sept 3, 1978

If you have kids going to school tomorrow you know this story well. It's about all the money you are shelling out for all those special notebooks, pens and crayons children are required to have at the beginning of school. They have to be exactly what the teacher specifies. Nothing else will do. It's always been that way as far back as I can remember. I've always been suspicious that teachers somehow get a kickback on these items. One year, when I was in grade school, a kid in our neighborhood passed out all these yellow pads that he got from his uncle's law office. But could we use them in school? Oh no. Not on your life. We had to have three ring paper with margins on either side. Years ago I taught school in a pretty tough neighborhood. If a kid could write a fairly interesting account of how he spent his summer vacation or if he could work out a complicated math problem, I was tickled if he wrote it on the back of an envelope or a piece of cardboard box. Traditionally, at the opening of the school year, we hear about a lot of things that have little to do with education. And in Chicago at the end of the school year we hear about all those children who don't know how to read. Just once I'd like to hear a kid come home from school after that first day and say: Ma, the teacher told us to bring a pencil and some paper tomorrow. We're going to learn how to read and write.

ABOUT THE AUTHOR

A native of Buffalo, NY, Peter Nolan began his broadcast career at WHLD Radio, Niagara Falls, NY. He also worked at WKBN-TV, Youngstown, Ohio before arriving in Chicago near the end of the turbulent 1960's where he worked in television news as a writer, reporter and commentator and won three Emmys and several journalism awards. His first book, CAMPAIGN! The 1983 Election that Rocked Chicago, was published in 2012 He lives in the Chicago suburb of Glenview.

ABOUT THE BACK COVER

The author being thanked by Mayor Richard J. Daley and the Chicago City Council for finding Rosemary Kennedy, sister of the late President, when she was lost for a short time in Chicago. October of 1975. The story is called A Missing Woman.

PHOTO SECTION

Msgr. Ignatius McDermott

The Angel of West Madison Street

Corneal Davis

Dean of the Illinois House

President John F. Kennedy

Shot down in Dallas Nov. 22, 1963

John Matijevich

Tried to repeal the Dram Shop law

Paul Adams

Principal who saved Providence-St. Mel High School

Fred Hubbard

Alderman with a gambling problem

Mayor Donald Stephens

The longest serving Mayor

Andrew McGann

kept calling the White House

Alderman Tom Keane

A Model Prisoner

Bobby Rush

The Black Panther who went to Congress

Jimmy Taylor

"I was just bull jiven em."

Bernie Epton

"He never got over the campaign of 1983"

Jimmy Hoffa

President Nixon freed him from prison

Michelle Clark

First female African American on network news

Otto Kerner

A Federal Judge and former Governor sent to prison

Sid Luckman

A Chicago Bears star meets a movie star

Charles "Chick" McCuen

The legendary NBC Newsman

Charles A. "Pat" Boyle with Pres. George H.W. Bush

The singing attorney

Jimmy Nolan

The loveable policeman who died too young

Roland Burris

Lincoln knew what happened in Illinois

St. Gabriel's Church

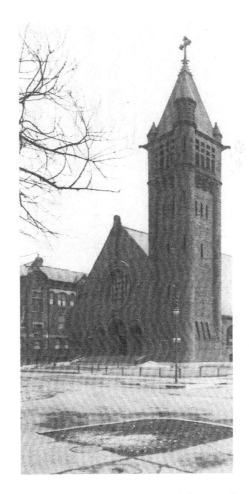

Father Dorney was King of the Yards

House of Bertini

John Rossi's restaurant on North Wells Street

Index

A

Abla Homes, 66, 69
Abraham Lincoln Hotel, 14, 15,
    204
Ackerman, Sergeant, 149-151
Adams, Paul, 62, 63, 221
African Americans
    and Altgeld Gardens, 45
    and Black Panther Party,
        117-119
    and Burris, 203, 204
    and Chicago Housing
        Authority, 65-70
    and Davis, 13-15
    and 18th ward, 52
    and Epton, 126-129
    and Hubbard, 80
    and Kerner Commission,
        132
    and Taylor, 121, 122
Allen, Walter, 76-78
Allstate Arena, 104
Altgeld Gardens, 46
American Falls, 24, 25
Anderson, John, 205, 206
Angel of West Madison
    Street. *See* McDermott,
    Monsignor Ignatius

Armstrong, Dwight, 57
Armstrong, Karlton, 57
Archdiocese of Chicago.
    See Roman Catholic
    Archdiocese of Chicago
Austin, Richard B., 68-70

B

Barsanti, John, 27, 31, 32
Battle, Melvin, 156
Bellino, June, 90
Benton, Joe, 96, 97
Better Government Association
    (BGA), 99-103
Black Panther Party, 67,
    117-119
Boyle, Pat, 155-157, 234
Brady, Danny, 38
Brady, Robert, 38
bribery
    and Daley, 51
    and fetcher bills, 54, 55
    and Kerner, 131
    and sludge, 93, 95, 96
    and Stephens, 102, 104
Brinkley, David, 137
Brownlee, Les, 81
Bull, Edwin, 95, 97

Burke, Ed, 182, 199
Burnham, Daniel, 166
Burris, Roland, 203, 204, 236
Burt, Leo, 57
Bush, George H. W., 209, 234
Byrne, Jane
  and Epton, 124, 125
  Illinois primary of 1980,
    199, 200
  and Taylor, 122

C
Cabrini-Green Homes, 66, 68
Campbell, William, 90
Canaryville, 165, 166
Capone, Al, 100, 185, 186
Carney, George, 86-88
Carpentersville, 29
Carr, Richard, 37
Carter, Jimmy, 96, 98, 199, 201,
    202, 205, 206
Casey, Bob, 27, 31, 32
Catholic Church. See Roman
    Catholic Archdiocese of
    Chicago
Channel 2 (CBS), 40, 41
Channel 5 (NBC)
  and American Falls, 25, 26
  commentaries on, 2, 78, 187
  coverage of Nixon, 176
  and FBI, 79-82
  and McCuen, 150-154
Channel 7 (ABC), 81
Chicago Bears, 141-144
Chicago City Council, 113, 114
Chicago Cubs, 65
Chicago Daily News, 48, 87

Chicago Housing Authority
    (CHA), 46, 65-70
Chicago Plan, 80
Chicago Police Department
  and Black Panthers, 117,
    118
  and Cohen, 35-38
  and Jimmy Nolan, 189,
    190
  and Loughnane, 83, 84
  and script pay, 181, 182
Chicago Sanitary District. See
    Metropolitan Sanitary
    District of Greater
    Chicago
Chicago Sun-Times, 48, 87,
    205
Chicago Today, 99, 100
Chicago Transit Authority
    (CTA), 161-163
Chicago Tribune, 82
Chicago Urban Transportation
    District, 205, 206
Chicago White Sox, 124
Ciccone, F. Richard, 152
City Savings and Loan scandal,
    89-91
Clan Na Gael, 167
Clark, Michelle, 137, 230
Cohen, Christopher, 37
Cohen, Jacob, 37, 38
Comito, Nick, 169
Cook County Democratic
    Central Committee,
    202
CTA. See Chicago Transit
    Authority

D
Daley, John, 51
Daley, Richard J., 199
    and Chicago Housing
        Authority, 69
    and Hanrahan, 118
    and Keane, 113
    and Kellam, 52
    and Matejevich, 55
Daley, Richard M., 125, 199
Danitz, Marcia, 41
Davis, Corneal A., 11-15, 204,
    218
D-Day, 43, 153, 154
Dedmon, Emmett, 48, 49
Democratic Machine
    and Kellam, 52, 53
    and Matejevich, 55
    selection of candidates, 128
    and Taylor, 121, 122
    and Washington, 125
Democratic Party
    and Hubbard, 80
    and Kellam, 51-53
    See Also Democratic
        Machine
Dorney, Maurice J., 166-168
dram shop law, 55, 56

E
Early, Sam, 86-88
East Dundee, 28
economy, 195
education, 61-64, 211
Elbert, Teddy, 177
el train derailment (1977),
    161-163

Epton, Bernie, 123-129, 228
Epton, Jeff, 128, 129

F
Fassnacht, Robert, 57
FBI (Federal Bureau of
    Investigation), 79-82, 96,
    103, 104
fetcher bill, 53-56
Fine, David, 57
fishing licenses, 71
Fitzpatrick, Tom, 87
Florida, 193, 194
Fulton County, 94

G
gangs, 66, 67
Gardner, Ava, 143, 144
Garrison, Bruce, 37
Gautreux v. Chicago Housing
    Authority, 65, 68
Genson, Edward, 83
Giancana, Sam, 101

H
Haider, Donald, 128
Halas, George, 142, 143
Hampton, Fred, 117-119
Hanrahan, Edward, 103, 118
Henry Horner Homes, 66
Hodges, Lee Arthur, 156
Hoffa, Jimmy, 137-139, 229
Hoffa, Jimmy, Jr., 139
Holliman, Greg, 68
Hollywood, 82, 143, 144
Houlihan, Mike, 68

House of Bertini Restaurant, 43
Hubbard, Fred, 80-82, 222

I
Illinois House of Representatives
and Davis, 12-14
and Epton, 123, 124
and fetcher bills, 53-56
and McGann, 110
and Taylor, 121, 122
Ingram, Bronson, 96, 97
Ingram, Frederick, 96-98

J
Jackson, Andrew, 40, 41
Janicki, Valentine, 93, 95, 97
Jenkins, Clara, 156
Jesse White Tumblers, 68
Johnson, Lyndon, 132, 176
Joliet Prison, 88
Joseph, Eddy, 20, 21

K
Keane, Thomas, 100, 113-115, 225
Kellam, Bob, 51, 52, 109
Kennedy, Jackie, 18
Kennedy, Joe, 18
Kennedy, John F.
assassination of, 17-22
and Austin, 69
and McGann, 110-112
photograph of, 219
Kennedy, Rosemary, 33, 34
Kennedy, Ted, 199-202

Kerner, Otto, 131-136, 231
Kerner Commission, 132
Koziol, Ron, 114, 115
Kupcinet, Irv, 141, 144

L
Lackey, E. Dent, 20
Lathrop Homes, 66
Lexington Hotel, 185, 186
Lincoln, Abraham, 203, 204
Loop, the, 161-163, 205
Loughnane, James, 83, 84
Loughnane, Michael, 83, 84
Luckman, Sid, 141-144, 232
Lueloff, Jorie, 3
Lyman, Bart, 95, 97

M
Machine, Democratic. *See* Democratic Machine
Madison, Wisconsin, 57-59
Mafia
and Capone, 100, 185, 186
and Rosemont, 99-101, 104
Mahoney, Tim, 29, 30
mail fraud, 114, 115
Majewski, Chester, 95, 97
Marovitz, Abe, 134-136
Marsek, William, 37
Marshall, Illinois, 183
Masterson, Frank, 39-41
Matejevich, John, 55, 220
McCarthy, Michael, 68
McCuen, Charles "Chick", 149-154, 233
McDermott, Monsignor Ignatius, 7-10, 217

McDonald's, 78
McGann, Andy, 51, 109-112, 224
McInerney and Sons, Thomas, 168
McIntire, Carl, 19
McMullen, Jay, 81
McNamee, Thom, 29, 30, 32
McNamee, Tim, 28-31
McPartlin, Robert, 95-98
Mensik, C. Orin, 89-91
Merchandise Mart, 18, 165
Metropolitan Sanitary District of Greater Chicago, 93-98
Miflin Street, 57-59
Migala, Lucyna, 2
Millhouse, Sylvia Ritter, 183
Mob, the. *See* Mafia
Mudd, Roger, 201
murder
    Loughnane case, 83, 84
    McNamee case, 28-32
    of policemen by Cohen, 35-38
    Price case, 155-157
    Speck case, 152, 153

N
Nally, Bill, 30, 31
Nash, Gordon, 97
NBC News Chicago. *See* WMAQ-TV Channel 5
Neal, Steve, 141
New Michigan Hotel. *See* Lexington Hotel
Niagara Falls (New York)

WHLD Radio, 17, 19-21, 23-25
Niagara Falls Gazette, 2, 24, 25
1960 Presidental Election, 17, 18
1980 Presidential Election, 201, 202
Nixon, Richard, 175-179
    and Hoffa, 138
    and Kennedy, 18
Nolan, Geraldine, 75-76
Nolan, Jimmy, 189, 190, 235
Nolan, Ralph W., 75, 76
None of the Above movement, 209
Noone, Anne, 68

O
Oakenwald School, 68
O'Brien, John, 82
O'Day, Stick, 197, 198
Olympia Fields Country Club, 69
Osborne, Alex, 145, 146
Osborne, John, 79, 82
Osborne, Russ, 145-147
Oster, Patrick, 100
Oswald, Lee Harvey, 21

P
Palmer, Arnold, 97
Palmer House, 47
Peebles, George, 72
Peoria, 152
Polikoff, Alexander, 69
Powell, Paul, 150, 151
Press, Valetta, 2

Price, Johnny, 155-157
prison
    free bus service to, 67
    and Keane, 114, 115
    and Kerner, 131
    and McPartlin, 97
    Stateville Prison Riot,
        85-88
Pritzker, A. N., 143
Providence St. Mel school,
    61-64
public housing. *See* Chicago
    Housing Authority
Pucinski, Roman, 201

Q
Quinlan, Mike, 78

R
Ramshaw, Greg, 100
Reagan, Ronald, 63, 125, 205,
    206
Rechtenwald, Bill, 100
Representatives, Illinois House
    of. *See* Illinois House of
    Representatives
Republican Party, 54, 56, 124,
    125, 128
Rhine River, 145-147
Rivera, Geraldo, 185, 186
Robert Taylor Homes, 66
Roman Catholic Archdiocese of
    Chicago
    Providence St. Mel, 61-64
    St. Gabriel's, 165-168
Rosemont, Illinois, 99-105,
    114

Roti, Fred, 80
Rossi, John, 43, 44
Rostenkowski, Dan, 96
Route 66 (TV show), 17
Royko, Mike, 87, 121, 173
Rubin, Harold, 186
Ruby, Jack, 21
Rush, Bobby, 117-119, 226
Ryan, George, 129

S
Saloom, Doris, 2
Samuels, Rich, 100
Sanitary District. *See*
    Metropolitan Sanitary
    District of Greater
    Chicago
Schmendera, Anthony, 90
school. *See* education
School, Back to, 211
Schultz, George, 47-50
Schultz, Mattie, 195
scotch whisky, 197, 198
script pay, 182
Secret Service, 112, 175, 177
Sielaff, Alyn, 86, 87
Skinner, Sam, 95, 96
Sludge, 93-98
Smith, Sandy, 101
snow, 171-173
Speck, Richard, 152, 153
Stateville Prison Riot, 85-88
Steele, John, 153, 154
Stephens, Brad, 104
Stephens, Donald, 99-105,
    223
Sterling Hall explosion, 57-59

St. Gabriel's Church, 165-68, 237
St. Mel's High School. *See* Providence St. Mel
St. Nicholas Hotel, 151
stockyards, 166, 167
Stricklin, Jim, 87
Strong, Jimmy, 141
Summerdale District, 35
Sun Bow Foundation, 186

T
Taylor, Jimmy "Bull Jive", 121, 122, 227
Teamsters Union, 138, 139
Terranova, Gaetano, 71-73
Terrorism, 57-59
Terryberry, Stan, 77
Thompson, Jim, 114
truck drivers, 207

V
Villanova University, 76, 79

W
Walker, Dan, 133
Walter, Nadine, 30-32

Washington, Harold
  and Davis, 13
  and Epton, 125-129
  and Taylor, 122
Watergate scandal, 48, 179
weather reporting, 171-173
Weber, Franklin, 95, 97
Wells Street, 43
whisky, 197, 198
White House, 110-112
White, Jesse, 68
WHLD Radio, 17, 19-21, 23-25, 76
Wimbish, C. C., 13, 14
wire services, 20
Wisconsin, University of, 57-59
WKBN TV Youngstown, 2, 25
WMAQ-TV. *See* Channel 5 (NBC)
World War II
  and Dedmon, 48
  and Epton, 123
  and Kerner, 132, 133
  and McCuen, 149, 150, 153, 154
  and McPartlin, 96
  and Osborne, 145-147
  and Rossi, 43, 44